LIVING THE QUESTIONS IN Mark

LIVING THE QUESTIONS IN Mark

A NavStudy Featuring *The* MESSAGE®

NAVPRESS®

BRINGING TRUTH TO LIFE

OUR GUARANTEE TO YOU

We believe so strongly in the message of our books that we are making this quality guarantee to you. If for any reason you are disappointed with the content of this book, return the title page to us with your name and address and we will refund to you the list price of the book. To help us serve you better, please briefly describe why you were disappointed. Mail your refund request to: NavPress, P.O. Box 35002, Colorado Springs, CO 80935.

© 2005 by The Navigators

ISBN 1-57683-860-9

Cover design by Disciple Design
Cover photo by Gary Walpole
Creative Team: Steve Parolini, Arvid Wallen, Kathy Mosier, Pat Reinheimer

Written and compiled by John Blase

Some of the anecdotal illustrations in this book are true to life and are included with the permission of the persons involved. All other illustrations are composites of real situations, and any resemblance to people living or dead is coincidental.

All Scripture quotations in this publication are taken from *THE MESSAGE* (MSG). Copyright © 1993, 1994, 1995, 1996, 2000, 2001, 2002. Used by permission of NavPress Publishing Group.

Printed in the United States of America

1 2 3 4 5 6 7 8 9 10 / 09 08 07 06 05

CONTENTS

I want to beg you, as much as I can . . . to be patient toward all that is unsolved in your heart and try to love the questions themselves like locked rooms and like books that are written in a very foreign tongue. Do not now seek the answers, which cannot be given you because you would not be able to live them. . . . Live the questions now. Perhaps you will then gradually, without noticing it, live along some distant day into the answer.

RAINER MARIA RILKE, *LETTERS TO A YOUNG POET*

Christians usually think about Jesus as the One with all the answers; the God-man with the evidence the verdict demands; a divine answer-man, sent down to earth to give us just what we need. And yes, he did give us just what we needed. Yet a careful reading of the Gospels shows that Jesus asked just as many questions as he gave outright answers. You would not have found a "The Bible says it, I believe it, and that settles it" bumper sticker on Jesus' backpack. It was more like, "This is God's Word. Stop and think about it, and let's talk about it."

However, the perception of Jesus as the divine answer-man appeals to a great many people. Life has questions, so you go to the Scriptures, look on the right page, find the answers, and everything's good. But while that works great for algebra class, it just doesn't seem to work well for this thing called *life*. Could the "divine answer-man" approach be too simplistic? Too one-dimensional for such a deep character as Jesus Christ? For one, it seems to leave you and me, the children of

God, out of the picture. We're not colaborers with God; we're just laborers.

Jesus went about doing good. Apparently part of this "good" was asking great questions—questions that would cause people to stop and pause and ponder the things they were living for and what might be worth dying for; questions not bound by a calendar but applicable to the ages; questions as poignant today as they were then.

The book you hold in your hand takes the approach of looking at the questions found in the Gospels—the questions Jesus asked. The questions are specific to the text of Eugene Peterson's *The Message*. I'm talking about questions such as, "All this time and money wasted on fashion—do you think it makes that much difference?" or "Who needs a doctor: the healthy or the sick?" Our temptation might be to respond quickly because we think we know the answers. But what if these questions must be lived? Lived out in dimensions such as friendship, family, and church? Lived out in locales such as homes, classrooms, and forests primeval? Lived by the flesh and blood whose main focus is the future, and lived by those who think mainly of the past? And what if living out these questions might lead us one day, gradually, without noticing it, into The Answer—the One who described himself as the way, truth, and life?

Live the questions now.

HOW TO USE THIS DISCUSSION GUIDE

1. This NavStudy is meant to be completed on your own *and* in a small group. You'll want to line up your study group ahead of time. A group of four to six is optimal—any bigger and one or more members will likely be shut out of discussions. Your small group can also be two. Each person will need his or her own copy of this book.

2. Lessons open with a Scripture passage intended to help you to prepare your heart and mind for the content that follows. Don't skip over this preparation time. Use it to reflect, slow down from a busy life, and transition into your study time.

3. *Read* the Scripture passages and other readings in each lesson. Let it all soak in. Re-read if necessary. There's no blue ribbon for finishing quickly. Make notes in the white space on the page. If you like journaling, think of this as a space to journal. If you don't like journaling, just think of it as space to "think out loud on paper."

4. *Think* about what you read. Respond to the questions we've provided. Always ask, "What does this mean?" and "Why does this matter?" about the readings. Compare different Bible translations for Scripture readings. Respond to the questions we've provided, and then discuss the questions when you're in your small group. Allow the experience of others to broaden your wisdom. You'll be stretched—called upon to evaluate what you've discovered and asked to make practical sense of it. In community, that stretching can often be painful and sometimes even embarrassing. But your willingness to be transparent—your openness to the possibility of personal growth—will reap great rewards.

5. *Pray* as you go through the entire session: before you read a word, in the middle of your thinking process, when you get stuck on a concept or passage, and as you approach the time when you'll explore

these passages and thoughts together in a small group. Pause when you need to ask God for inspiration or when you need to cry out in frustration. Compose a prayer prompted by what you've uncovered in the readings and your responses to the "Think" questions.

6. *Live.* (That's "live" as in "rhymes with give" as in "Give me something I can really use in my life.") This is a place to choose one thing you can do to live out the question posed in the lesson. Don't try to craft a plan that is lofty or unreachable. Choose something small, something doable. Then, in your small group, talk about this "one thing." Commit to following through on your idea, wrestle with what that means in practical terms, and call upon your group members to hold you accountable.

7. *Follow up.* Don't let the life application drift away without action. Be accountable to small-group members and refer to previous "Live" as in "rhymes with give" sections often. Take time at the beginning of each new study to review. See how you're doing.

SMALL-GROUP STUDY TIPS

After going through each week's study on your own, it's time to sit down with others and go deeper. Here are a few thoughts on how to make the most of your small-group discussion time.

Set ground rules. You don't need many. Here are two:

First, you'll want group members to make a commitment to the entire ten-week study. Significant personal growth happens when group members spend enough time together to really get to know each other. Hit-and-miss attendance can hinder this growth.

Second, agree together that everyone's story is important. Time is a valuable commodity, so if you have an hour to spend together, do your best to give each person ample time to express concerns, pass along insights, and generally feel like a participating member of the group. Small-group discussions are not monologues. However, a one-person-dominated discussion isn't always a bad thing. Not only is your role in a small group to explore and expand your own understanding, it's also to support one another. If someone truly needs more of the floor, give it to him or her. There will be times when the needs of the one outweigh the needs of the many. Use good judgment and allow extra space when needed. *Your* time might be next week.

Meet regularly. Choose a time and place, and stick to it. Consistency removes stress that could otherwise frustrate discussion and subsequent personal growth.

Follow the book outline. Each week, open your small-group time with prayer, and read aloud the reflective Scripture passage that opens the lesson. Then go through the study together, reading each section aloud and discussing it with your group members. Tell others what you wrote. Write down new insights gleaned from other group members. Wrestle the questions together. When you get to the "Pray" section, ask for volunteers willing to read aloud their written prayers. Finally, spend a few minutes talking together about each person's "one thing" and how to achieve that goal.

Talk openly. If you enter this study with shields up, you're probably not alone. And you're not a "bad person" for your hesitation to unpack your life in front of friends or strangers. Maybe you're skeptical about the value of revealing to others the deepest parts of who you are. Maybe you're simply too afraid of what might fall out of the suitcase. You don't have to go to a place where you're uncomfortable. If you want to sit and listen, offer a few thoughts, or even express a surface level of your own pain, go ahead. But don't neglect what brings you to this place—that longing for meaning. You can't ignore it away. Dip your feet in the water of brutally honest discussion, and you may choose to dive in. There is healing here.

Stay on task. Refrain from sharing material that falls into the "too much information" category. Don't spill unnecessary stuff. If structure isn't your group's strength, try a few minutes of general comments about the study, and then take each question one at a time and give everyone in the group a chance to respond.

"What kind of action suits the Sabbath best?
Doing good or doing evil?" (Mark 3:4)

Before You Begin

Take some time to reflect and prepare your heart and mind
for this study. Read the following Scripture passage. Soak
up God's Word. There's no hurry. Then, when you're ready,
turn the page and begin.

Exodus 20:8-11

Observe the Sabbath day, to keep it holy. Work six days and
do everything you need to do. But the seventh day is
a Sabbath to God, your God. Don't do any work—not
you, nor your son, nor your daughter, nor your servant,
nor your maid, nor your animals, not even the foreign
guest visiting in your town. For in six days God made
Heaven, Earth, and sea, and everything in them; he
rested on the seventh day. Therefore God blessed the
Sabbath day; he set it apart as a holy day.

READ

Mark 2:23–3:6

One Sabbath day he was walking through a field of ripe grain. As his disciples made a path, they pulled off heads of grain. The Pharisees told on them to Jesus: "Look, your disciples are breaking Sabbath rules!"

Jesus said, "Really? Haven't you ever read what David did when he was hungry, along with those who were with him? How he entered the sanctuary and ate fresh bread off the altar, with the Chief Priest Abiathar right there watching—holy bread that no one but priests were allowed to eat—and handed it out to his companions?" Then Jesus said, "The Sabbath was made to serve us; we weren't made to serve the Sabbath. The Son of Man is no lackey to the Sabbath. He's in charge!"

Then he went back in the meeting place where he found a man with a crippled hand. The Pharisees had their eyes on Jesus to see if he would heal him, hoping to catch him in a Sabbath infraction. He said to the man with the crippled hand, "Stand here where we can see you."

Then he spoke to the people: "**What kind of action suits the Sabbath best? Doing good or doing evil?** Helping people or leaving them helpless?" No one said a word.

He looked them in the eye, one after another, angry now, furious at their hard-nosed religion. He said to the man, "Hold out your hand." He held it out—it was as good as new! The Pharisees got out as fast as they could, sputtering about how they would join forces with Herod's followers and ruin him.

THINK "What kind of action suits the Sabbath best? Doing good or doing evil?"

- What is your immediate response to this question?
- Why do you think you responded in this way?

• Read the introductory passage from Exodus again and then put yourself in the Pharisees' sandals for a moment. Do you empathize with them at all?

• At one point Jesus is described as "angry" and "furious." How do those descriptions affect your reading of these words?

• Ponder this for a moment: Jesus says that the Sabbath (usually viewed as a day of rest) can be characterized by action (usually thought of as nonrest). What is your reaction to that seeming paradox?

READ

From *Spiritual Friend*, by Tilden Edwards[1]

Today, in the Protestant-dominated parts of the West especially, we are pulling away from the last vestiges of a well-intentioned but oppressively legalistic period of Christian Sabbath observance. Sunday legislation probably reached its height of narrow, rigid interpretation in the English Puritans' seventeenth-century legislative acts that prohibited any kind of recreation on Sunday, even going for a walk.

With the gradual demise of the last related "Blue Laws" legislation in the United States, there is a general sigh of relief. On the other hand, with them one of the few remaining symbols of a meaningful basic rhythm of life has been abolished from public consciousness. As Harvey Cox says, though Sunday is a holiday, it increasingly is just another day whose emptiness is filled with leisure industries. The Churches themselves increasingly are limited to a rushed hour of vestigial Sabbath gathering, with no sense of a whole day's different rhythm of life. Numerous non-observant Jews ignore the Sabbath altogether. Liberal Jews can water it down to a glancing tip of the hat, along with a majority of Christians. For others in the culture, the Sabbath is simply unheard of.

What are we missing in ignoring the guidance of this different quality of time represented by the Sabbath? We are missing a profound human truth: our need for what the great Jewish scholar and mystic, Abraham Joshua Heschel, called "a sanctuary—a cathedral in time."

THINK   "What kind of action suits the Sabbath best? Doing good or doing evil?"

- What was your experience of Sabbath growing up? Narrow and rigid? Watered down? Simply unheard of?
- Who or what primarily influenced that experience?

- What role does Sabbath play in your life now?
- Edwards talks of a "meaningful basic rhythm of life." Do you believe there is such a thing? Why or why not?
- How does the offer of "a sanctuary—a cathedral in time" sound to you?
- What would you do in your "cathedral"?

READ

From *Making Sunday Special*, by Karen Mains[2]

I would hustle and bustle, find the missing shoe, iron the shirt that had been neglected the night before, throw the wet clothes into the dryer, set the table for ten for Sunday dinner, prepare a simple meal for guests, go over the last-minute preparations for our interracial Christian Education Center plans, then finally get myself dressed after a most inadequate catch-as-catch-can family breakfast. David would emerge from his study, holiness sitting on his brow, anointed to present the Word of the Lord to our congregation, oozing peace and equanimity. Oh yes, I knew how Martha felt when Mary sat at the feet of Jesus.

But then I discovered that many Christian families (not just those of us in pastoral ministry) had the same struggles. Sunday morning, leaving for church, was often the worst time in their week.

As a couple, David and I vowed to work together to restore our observance of the Lord's Day, to seek to make Sunday the best day of the week, the high point, to struggle to establish this rhythm of the sacred in our lives as individuals and in our lives as a family. We wanted Sunday to become the joyful focal point of our weekly lives.

Now it's important to underline the word joyful. We did not want to slip back into an old legalism, that grim old joyless observance of the Lord's Day with its killing *can'ts* and *don'ts* and *won'ts* and *shall nots*. That attitude has done as much to create a dread of worship as anything I know. It was against this kind of legalism Christ had to continually speak. In three of the Gospels his words of reminder and rebuke are recorded, "The Sabbath was made for man, not man for the Sabbath." I wanted the kind of celebration in our family hearts that I read about in Isaiah . . .

> "If you . . . call the Sabbath a *delight* . . . if you honor it,
> not going your own ways . . . then you shall take delight
> in the Lord . . ." (Isaiah 58:13-14).

So David and I moved slowly but determinedly into recapturing Sunday meaningfulness in our new role as lay people. We refused to schedule meetings on Saturday evenings. If we were traveling, we attempted to return home in time for church on Sunday. . . . Not only were we going absolutely counter to the secular culture of society in which the weekend was viewed hedonistically and narcissistically, but we soon discovered that we were going counter to the secularized culture of the church where a full calendar was viewed as sacred.

THINK
"What kind of action suits the Sabbath best? Doing good or doing evil?"

- Can you relate to what Mains says about her Sunday mornings?
- Would you use the words *joyful* and *delight* to describe your Sabbath experiences?
- Have you been or are you now a part of the church culture that sees a full calendar as sacred?
- If you want to change your current experience, how would you go about doing that?

READ

From *Community and Growth*, by Jean Vanier[3]

Many people get burned out because, perhaps unconsciously, some part of them is rejecting the need to relax and find a harmonious rhythm of life for themselves. In their over-activity they are fleeing from something, sometimes because of deep unconscious guilt feelings. Maybe they do not really want to put down roots in the community and stay for the long haul. They may be too attached to their function, perhaps even identified with it. They want to control everything, and perhaps even want to appear to be perfect, or at least a perfect hero! They have not yet learned how to live; they are not yet free inside themselves; they have not yet discovered the wisdom of the present moment, which can frequently mean saying "no" to people.

These people need a spiritual guide to help them look at themselves and discover why they have not the freedom to stop, and what is the cause of their compulsive need to do things. They need someone who can help them stand back and relax enough to clarify their own motives and become people living with other people, children among other children. God has given each of us an intelligence. It may not be very great, but it is great enough for us to reflect on what we need in order to live what we are called to live—community.

THINK "What kind of action suits the Sabbath best? Doing good or doing evil?"

- Does this passage change in any way the way you've been thinking about Jesus' question?
- What are your reactions to the idea that relaxed people are best able to do good or truly help people?
- Would you describe yourself as a person who can stop and rest? Or do you have a "compulsive need to do things"?

• Would others around you agree with your answer to the previous question?

READ

From *Keeping the Sabbath Wholly*, by Marva Dawn[4]

One of the specific choices among the values of the Christian community is the embracing of time instead of space. We must return to the question of how we in our busy lives can afford to spend a whole day in Sabbath ceasing, resting, embracing, and feasting when it seems we don't have enough time to do what has to be done. Surrounded as we are by the rapid pace of too much change, we think we cannot set aside such time. However, when we take the day to assess our use of time, we learn what is important in all those changes and how to prioritize our tasks and desires so that we aren't overcome by the tyranny of the urgent. We must develop an objective perspective . . . to assess the quality of our days. This perspective has many aspects, but one of the foremost is the deliberate decision to focus on events in time with persons rather than using time to acquire or accomplish things.

THINK   "What kind of action suits the Sabbath best? Doing good or doing evil?"

- When was the last time you took a Sabbath and assessed your use of time?
- Can you recall a Sabbath (Sunday) that was overtaken by the "tyranny of the urgent"? What was that like?
- Later in her book, Dawn refers to the Sabbath as "a day to celebrate persons and life." How does that sound to you? What would it take for you to move in that direction?

PRAY

Look back at the "Think" sections. Ruminate on your responses. Let them distill into a prayer, and then write that prayer below.

Lord of the Sabbath . . .

The issue of prayer is not prayer; the issue of prayer is God.

ABRAHAM HESCHEL

LIVE   "What kind of action suits the Sabbath best? Doing
good or doing evil?"

The challenge now is to take this question further along—to live out
this question. Think of one thing, *just one*, that you can personally
do to wrestle with the question, inhabit the character of it, and live
it in everyday life. In the following space, jot down your thoughts on
this "one thing." Read the quotes that follow for additional inspiration. During the coming week, pray about this "one thing," talk with a
close friend about it, and learn to live the question.

One thing . . .

Six days we live under the tyranny of things in space; on
the Sabbath we try to become attuned to holiness in time,
a day on which we are called . . . to turn from the results to
the mystery of creation; from the world of creation to the
creation of the world.

Abraham Heschel

My Lord Sabbath
Welcome to my home.
Welcome to my heart.
Welcome to my mind.
Welcome to my spirit.
May this Sabbath/Sunday
Be filled with your presence.
Amen.

Live the questions now. Perhaps you will then gradually, without
noticing it, live along some distant day into the answer.
RAINER MARIA RILKE, *LETTERS TO A YOUNG POET*

LESSON 2

"How can we picture God's kingdom?
What kind of story can we use?" (Mark 4:30)

Before You Begin

Take some time to reflect and prepare your heart and mind
for this study. Read the following Scripture passage. Soak
up God's Word. There's no hurry. Then, when you're ready,
turn the page and begin.

Psalm 78:1-4

Listen, dear friends, to God's truth,
　　bend your ears to what I tell you.
I'm chewing on the morsel of a proverb;
　　I'll let you in on the sweet old truths,
Stories we heard from our fathers,
　　counsel we learned at our mother's knee.
We're not keeping this to ourselves,
　　we're passing it along to the next generation—
God's fame and fortune,
　　the marvelous things he has done.

READ

Mark 4:1-2,26-34

He went back to teaching by the sea. A crowd built up to such a great size that he had to get into an offshore boat, using the boat as a pulpit as the people pushed to the water's edge. He taught by using stories, many stories. . . .

Then Jesus said, "God's kingdom is like seed thrown on a field by a man who then goes to bed and forgets about it. The seed sprouts and grows—he has no idea how it happens. The earth does it all without his help: first a green stem of grass, then a bud, then the ripened grain. When the grain is fully formed, he reaps—harvest time!

"**How can we picture God's kingdom? What kind of story can we use?** It's like a pine nut. When it lands on the ground it is quite small as seeds go, yet once it is planted it grows into a huge pine tree with thick branches. Eagles nest in it."

With many stories like these, he presented his message to them, fitting the stories to their experience and maturity. He was never without a story when he spoke. When he was alone with his disciples, he went over everything, sorting out the tangles, untying the knots.

THINK   "How can we picture God's kingdom? What kind of story can we use?"

- What is your immediate response to this question?
- Why do you think you responded in this way?
- Is there someone in your life you would consider a storyteller? What is your opinion of that person?
- Is "storyteller" one of the images you have of Jesus? Why or why not?
- Think about this statement: "He was never without a story when he spoke." What does this say to you?

THINK (continued)

READ

From *The Clown in the Belfry*, by Frederick Buechner[1]

Jesus did not say that religion was the truth or that his own teachings were the truth or that what people taught about him was the truth or that the Bible was the truth or the Church or any system of ethics or theological doctrine. There are individual truths in all of them, we hope and believe, but individual truths were not what Pilate was after or what you and I are after either unless I miss my guess. Truths about this or that are a dime a dozen, including religious truths. THE truth is what Pilate is after: the truth about who we are and who God is if there is a God, the truth about life, the truth about death, the truth about truth itself. That is the truth we are all of us after.

It is a truth that can never be put into words because no words can contain it. It is a truth that can never be caught in any doctrine or creed including our own because it will never stay still long enough but is always moving and shifting like air. It is a truth that is always beckoning us in different ways and coming at us from different directions. And I think that is precisely why whenever Jesus tries to put that ultimate and inexpressible truth into words (instead of into silence as he did with Pilate) the form of words he uses is a form that itself moves and shifts and beckons us in different ways and comes at us from different directions. That is to say he tells stories.

Jesus does not sound like Saint Paul or Thomas Aquinas or John Calvin when we hear him teaching in the Gospels. "Once upon a time" is what he says. Once upon a time somebody went out to plant seeds. Once upon a time somebody stubbed a toe on a great treasure. Once upon a time somebody lost a precious coin. The Gospels are full of the stories Jesus tells, stories that are alive in somewhat the way the truth is alive, the way he himself is alive when Pilate asks him about truth, and his silence is a way of saying, "Look at my aliveness if you want to know! Listen to my life!" Matthew goes so far as to tell us that "he said nothing to them without a parable," that is to say without a story, and then quotes the words, "I will open my mouth in parables, I will utter what has been hidden since the foundation of the world." In stories the hiddenness and the utterance are both present, and that is another reason why they are a good way of talking about God's truth which is part hidden and part uttered too.

THINK   "How can we picture God's kingdom? What kind of story can we use?"

- What feelings or thoughts do Buechner's words stir in you?
- Do you enjoy Jesus' stories, or parables, in the Gospels? Why or why not?
- Which of Jesus' stories have had the most impact on your life? Why do you think you connect with these particular stories?
- In what ways do you use stories to share what you believe with others?

READ

From *Ragman and Other Cries of Faith*, by Walter Wangerin Jr.[2]

Abstraction, . . . the removing of God from experiential life and permitting him truly to dwell in the analysis alone, is a present-day problem. To be sure, the Greeks of the fifth century B.C.—those who poo-pooed the historical value of their myths, re-interpreting them and worshiping the wisdom which triumphed over story—had mentalized their gods as well; but these were a clear minority and the rest of the culture continued to offer sacrifice. Today the trouble's more pervasive for two reasons: first, we are less honest than they. We pretend God's presence in the whole of our lives, and we believe the pretence, though in fact we honor understanding. Second, our priests themselves participate in the problem. Because they are also preachers; because so many of us consider preaching to be their most significant function; preaching seems to us the clearest access to the divine. Therefore, the shape of preaching most shapes our God. And what is the shape of most preaching today? Why, it is the shape of the classroom: teaching. And teaching is always (in our consideration) one step removed from experience and from the "real." It is an activity of the mind. It prepares for what will be; or it interprets what has been; it is separated from both. The God who is met in doctrines, who is apprehended in the catechesis, who is true so long as our statements about him are truly stated, who is communicated in propositions, premise-premise-conclusion, who leaps not from the streets, nor even from the scriptural texts, but from the interpretation of the scriptural texts—that God is an abstract, has been abstracted from the rest of the Christian's experience.

THINK   "How can we picture God's kingdom? What kind of story can we use?"

- Wangerin states that the shape of most preaching today is "the shape of the classroom: teaching." Think about the shape of most of the preaching you have been exposed to in your life. Would you say most of it was storytelling or teaching?

- Have there been moments while listening to sermons when you thought it all seemed "one step removed from experience"? If so, why did it seem that way?

- Wangerin says that the Greeks had "mentalized" their gods. Do you think that could be said about Christians in America today? Why or why not?

- What steps can be taken to change the abstraction of God into a reality?

READ

From *Waking the Dead*, by John Eldredge[3]

Think of it. You are the Son of the living God. You have come to earth to rescue the human race. It is your job to communicate truths without which your precious ones will be lost . . . forever. Would you do it like this? Really now. A treasure hidden in a field? A lump of dough? Ten virgins and something about oil? Why doesn't he come right out and say it—get to the point? What's with all the stories? Some of them rather puzzling, I might add. Jesus is not entertaining children; he is speaking to adults about the deepest things in life. And I think it's safe to say he knows quite well what he's doing. As Dallas Willard reminds us, Jesus is brilliant. He is the smartest man who ever lived. So what's up with all the stories?

We children of the Internet and the cell phone and the Weather Channel, we think we are the enlightened ones. We aren't fooled by anything—we just want the facts. The bottom line. So proposition has become our means of saying what is true and what is not. And proposition is helpful . . . for certain things. Sacramento is the capital of California; water freezes at 32 degrees Fahrenheit; your shoes are in the front room, under the sofa. But proposition fails when it comes to the weightier things in life. While it is a fact that the Civil War was fought between the years of 1861 and 1865 and while it is also a fact that hundreds of thousands of men died in that war, those facts hardly describe what happened at Bull Run or Antietam, at Cold Harbor or Gettysburg. You don't even begin to grasp the reality of the Civil War until you hear the stories, see pictures from the time, visit the battlefields, watch a film like *Glory*.

How much more so when it comes to the deep truths of the Christian faith. God loves you; you matter to him. That is a fact, stated as a proposition. I imagine most of you have heard it any number of times. Why, then, aren't we the happiest people on earth? It hasn't reached our hearts. Facts stay lodged in the mind, for the most part. They don't speak at the level we need to hear. Proposition speaks to the mind, but when you tell a story, you speak to the heart. We've been telling each other stories since the beginning of time. It is our way of communicating the timeless truths, passing them down.

And that's why when Jesus comes to town, he speaks in a way that will get past all our intellectual defenses and disarm our hearts. He tells a certain kind of story. . . . And the best stories of all, the ones that bring us the Eternal Truths, they always take the form of parable or, sometimes we say, fairy tale. Better still to call them myths. . . . And I've already lost many of you. For most of us rationalists, the word means "not true." Isn't that what you think when you hear someone say, "Oh, that's just a myth"? Meaning, that's not factually true. But myth is a story, like a parable, that speaks of Eternal Truths. . . . Christian professor Rolland Hein has described it this way: "Myths are, first of all, stories: stories which confront us with something transcendent and eternal . . . a means by which the eternal expresses itself in time."

THINK "How can we picture God's kingdom? What kind of story can we use?"

- Write down some initial reactions to this passage. Don't evaluate; just react.
- Do you feel there is any validity to what Eldredge is saying? Why or why not?
- Did you have any negative reactions to the passage? What were they, and why did they strike you that way?
- Is there a story, movie, film, or piece of music that has confronted you lately with something "transcendent and eternal"? Think about why it spoke to you.

THINK (continued)

READ

From *Reflections on the Movies*, by Ken Gire[4]

As the queen leaves, the camera focuses on Arthur's face. He is regal in his reserve, resolved to be a king and not a man. Yet it is a man's heart that is broken. And it is a man's words that are spoken. The words, spoken softly to himself, are as tender as they are tragic.

"Good-bye, my love . . . my dearest love."

The pain you feel for him, for all of them, is too great to bear without the shoulders of tears. The king stands for a moment in silence until Guenevere is gone, then is jostled out of his silence by a rustling sound behind a nearby tent.

"Who's there? Who's there? Come out, I say!"

A frightened young boy, no older than twelve, emerges from behind the tent: "Forgive me, Your Majesty. I was searching for the sergeant of arms and got lost. I didn't wish to disturb you."

"Who are you, boy? Where did you come from? You ought to be in bed. Are you a page?"

"I stowed away on one of the boats, Your Majesty. I came to fight for the Round Table. I'm very good with the bow."

"And do you think you will kill people with this bow of yours?"

"Oh yes, Milord. A great many, I hope."

"Suppose they kill you?"

"Then I shall be dead, Milord. But I don't intend to be dead. I intend to be a knight."

"A knight?"

"Yes, Milord. Of the Round Table."

"When did you decide upon this nonexistent career? Was your village protected by knights when you were a small boy? Was your mother saved by a knight? Did your father serve as a knight?"

"Oh no, Milord. I had never seen a knight until I stowed away. I only know of them. The stories people tell."

"From the stories people tell you wish to be a knight?"

THINK "How can we picture God's kingdom? What kind of story can we use?"

- What is your initial reaction to this passage?
- Think about the evangelistic efforts you have been a part of or have experienced in some way. Were they more story focused or statement focused (points, propositions, and so on)?
- If they were statement focused, do you believe they caused anyone to wish to be a follower of Christ? Why or why not?

PRAY

Look back at the "Think" sections. Ruminate on your responses. Let them distill into a prayer, and then write that prayer below.

Author and Finisher of all life . . .

The issue of prayer is not prayer; the issue of prayer is God.

ABRAHAM HESCHEL

LIVING THE QUESTIONS SERIES

LIVE

"How can we picture God's kingdom? What kind of story can we use?"

The challenge now is to take this question further along—to live out this question. Think of one thing, *just one*, that you can personally do to wrestle with the question, inhabit the character of it, and live it in everyday life. In the following space, jot down your thoughts on this "one thing." Read the quotes that follow for additional inspiration. During the coming week, pray about this "one thing," talk with a close friend about it, and learn to live the question.

One thing . . .

I love the ability to tell a story and to tell it well. Traditionally, wealth was often determined by your gifts in this area. How many songs do you know? How many stories can you tell? And how well can you tell them? I think the skills which enabled the retelling of memory were seen as our true riches.

Joy Harjo

Some writers whom I admire very much say that facts often have little to do with the truth.

Carolyn Forche

Live the questions now. Perhaps you will then gradually, without noticing it, live along some distant day into the answer.

RAINER MARIA RILKE, *LETTERS TO A YOUNG POET*

"Why are you such cowards? Don't you have any faith at all?"

(Mark 4:40)

Before You Begin

Take some time to reflect and prepare your heart and mind for this study. Read the following Scripture passage. Soak up God's Word. There's no hurry. Then, when you're ready, turn the page and begin.

MARK 5:32-34

But he went on asking, looking around to see who had done it. The woman, knowing what had happened, knowing she was the one, stepped up in fear and trembling, knelt before him, and gave him the whole story.

Jesus said to her, "Daughter, you took a risk of faith, and now you're healed and whole. Live well, live blessed! Be healed of your plague."

READ

Mark 4:35-41

> Late that day he said to them, "Let's go across to the other side." They took him in the boat as he was. Other boats came along. A huge storm came up. Waves poured into the boat, threatening to sink it. And Jesus was in the stern, head on a pillow, sleeping! They roused him, saying, "Teacher, is it nothing to you that we're going down?"
>
> Awake now, he told the wind to pipe down and said to the sea, "Quiet! Settle down!" The wind ran out of breath; the sea became smooth as glass. Jesus reprimanded the disciples: **"Why are you such cowards? Don't you have any faith at all?"**
>
> They were in absolute awe, staggered. "Who is this, anyway?" they asked. "Wind and sea at his beck and call!"

THINK   "Why are you such cowards? Don't you have any faith at all?"

- What is your immediate response to this question?
- Why do you think you responded in this way?
- Think back to when you first heard this story. How do you recall it?
- Think about Jesus' words to the disciples. The text says he "reprimanded" them. What do you see going on here? (Don't overlook what the disciples asked: "Teacher, is it nothing to you that we're going down?")
- What might have happened if the disciples hadn't roused Jesus from his nap?

THINK (continued)

READ

Psalm 91

> You who sit down in the High God's presence,
>   spend the night in Shaddai's shadow,
> Say this: "GOD, you're my refuge.
>   I trust in you and I'm safe!"
> That's right—he rescues you from hidden traps,
>   shields you from deadly hazards.
> His huge outstretched arms protect you—
>   under them you're perfectly safe;
>   his arms fend off all harm.
> Fear nothing—not wild wolves in the night,
>   not flying arrows in the day,
> Not disease that prowls through the darkness,
>   not disaster that erupts at high noon.
> Even though others succumb all around,
>   drop like flies right and left,
>   no harm will even graze you.
> You'll stand untouched, watch it all from a distance,
>   watch the wicked turn into corpses.
> Yes, because GOD's your refuge,
>   the High God your very own home,
> Evil can't get close to you,
>   harm can't get through the door.
> He ordered his angels
>   to guard you wherever you go.
> If you stumble, they'll catch you;
>   their job is to keep you from falling.
> You'll walk unharmed among lions and snakes,
>   and kick young lions and serpents from the path.
>
> "If you'll hold on to me for dear life," says GOD,
>   "I'll get you out of any trouble.
> I'll give you the best of care

if you'll only get to know and trust me.
Call me and I'll answer, be at your side in bad times;
I'll rescue you, then throw you a party.
I'll give you a long life,
give you a long drink of salvation!"

THINK   "Why are you such cowards? Don't you have any faith at all?"

- Read the psalm again slowly. Underline significant phrases or words.
- Does this psalm line up with your life experience so far? Have you been kept "perfectly safe"? Have you stood "untouched"? Has evil not been able to "get close to you"? Have you walked "unharmed among lions and snakes"?
- If there are some discrepancies, what's going on here?
- How often do these words leave your lips: "GOD, you're my refuge. I trust in you"? Seldom? Fairly often? Frequently? Daily?

READ

From *Life Can Begin Again*, by Helmut Thielicke[1]

If there were *one* point at which I could see that there is a living heart that beats for this world, then my anxiety would be removed with one blow. Then nothing could touch me that had not first passed the censorship of that heart and been declared by that heart to be wholesome and good for me. Then in everything that troubles me, in everything I dread the hidden theme of love is at work, even though I am unable to detect it in the confused beat of this disjointed world. Then for me it would simply be enough that all these things come from the heart of God and are meant to lead me back to him.

And this one point at which this tremendous liberating comfort and assurance becomes visible and available to me is Jesus Christ. I have used the illustration of the magnifying glass before. Only if we look through the middle of the glass do we see the object behind more sharply and clearly. The farther we move away from it and the more our eyes are focused on the edges of the glass, the more distorted and unrecognizable the object becomes. And the same is true of the way that Jesus Christ helps us to look at life. Only if we view the mystery of life through him, through the Center of history, does it gain its old clarity; for when we look through him we are looking into the heart of God. But the farther we move away from this Center and allow our eyes to wander to the edges the more distorted, impenetrable and satanic becomes everything that comes into our field of vision. At the margins the anxiety of life prevails. Only at the center, the focus, only in Jesus Christ do I see the Father and what he wills for me. . . .

The opposite of care is therefore not the kind of optimism that persuades itself that everything is not so bad after all, that things will straighten out somehow. The so-called optimists on principle are generally mere windbags, superficial characters who are not serious or courageous enough to face the realities.

Rather, the opposite of care is *faith*. It is the faith that knows the uncertainty of the future and faces all the enigmas and seemingly meaningless events of life. It simply says, "Nevertheless I am continually with thee."

I beg you to note that faith does not say, "Nevertheless I will remain standing; 'what does not get me down makes me stronger.'" Any lout could say that, if the size of his brain did not prevent him from thinking a philosophical thought. No; faith says, "Perhaps I may fall and often I am helpless, but thou wilt lift me up. My understanding is staggered and utterly confused in the face of the great mass of suffering in the world, but thou dost not forsake me, and therefore I too will hold fast to thy hand. For I know that thy love has its way even in the deepest darkness." This is the sense in which faith is the opposite of care. And this is how the Lord himself expressed it when he said, "Do not fear, only believe" (Mark 5:36).

Once we allow God to give us this trust, then we begin to taste something of the royal freedom of the children of God and, mysteriously, our whole attitude toward the future changes. Our first interest is no longer the question (the frightened, despairing question) whether God will help, but rather that other question (the glad, confident, eagerly curious question) *how* God will help. Pascal once said that it is glorious to ride on a ship in stormy weather when one knows that it cannot go down.

THINK   "Why are you such cowards? Don't you have any faith at all?"

- How does this passage make you feel?
- What is causing you anxiety in your life right now?
- Think about Thielicke's statement: "At the margins the anxiety of life prevails. Only at the center, the focus, only in Jesus Christ do I see the Father and what he wills for me." Are you looking at life through the margins? Or are you looking through the Center, Jesus Christ?

- Spend some time soaking up this thought: "Our first interest is no longer the question (the frightened, despairing question) whether God will help, but rather that other question (the glad, confident, eagerly curious question) *how* God will help."

READ

From *The Journey of Desire*, by John Eldredge[2]

Virtually every person I've ever counseled follows a similar pattern. Over the course of our time together, some wonderful things begin to happen. Not necessarily at first, and never on command, but God shows up. The lights turn on for these people; their heart is lifted; grateful tears flow. Suddenly, faith, hope, and love seem the only way to live. And I nearly dread the next session. When they return the following week, it is as though it never happened. The marvelous day is a distant memory. Life is hard, God is distant, and love is foolish. All is forgotten; all is sick-heart vanity. I want to grab them and shake them into sense, shouting, "Don't you *remember*? Why did you let it slip away?" Wisdom has restrained me so far.

Forgetting is no small problem. Of all the enemies our hearts must face, this may be the worst because it is insidious. Forgetfulness does not come against us like an enemy in full battle formation, banners waving. Nor does it come temptingly, seductively, the lady in red. It works slowly, commonly, unnoticed. My wife had a beautiful climbing rose vine that began to fill an arbor in her garden. We enjoyed the red blossoms it produced every summer. But last year, something happened. The vine suddenly turned brown, dropped its flowers, and died within the course of a week. After all that loving care we couldn't figure out what went wrong. A call to the nursery revealed that a worm had gotten into the stalk of the vine and eaten away at the life from the inside. Such is the work of forgetfulness. It cuts us off from our Life so slowly, we barely notice, until one day the blooms of our faith are suddenly gone.

THINK   "Why are you such cowards? Don't you have any faith at all?"

- Have you ever considered forgetfulness to be an enemy of your soul? Why or why not?
- What are some things God has graciously done for you?
- Is your faith blooming or withering right now?
- Spend some time recounting the wondrous works of God. As the old hymn says, "Count your blessings, name them one by one."

PRAY

Look back at the "Think" sections. Ruminate on your responses. Let them distill into a prayer, and then write that prayer below.

Jesus, be my Center . . .

The issue of prayer is not prayer; the issue of prayer is God.

Abraham Heschel

LIVE

"Why are you such cowards? Don't you have any faith at all?"

The challenge now is to take this question further along—to live out this question. Think of one thing, *just one*, that you can personally do to wrestle with the question, inhabit the character of it, and live it in everyday life. In the following space, jot down your thoughts on this "one thing." Read the Scripture and quotes that follow for additional inspiration. During the coming week, pray about this "one thing," talk with a close friend about it, and learn to live the question.

One thing . . .

Just make sure you stay alert. Keep close watch over yourselves. Don't forget anything of what you've seen. Don't let your heart wander off. Stay vigilant as long as you live. Teach what you've seen and heard to your children and grandchildren.

Deuteronomy 4:9

And so we revolted against silence with a bit of speaking.

Carolyn Forche

Live the questions now. Perhaps you will then gradually, without noticing it, live along some distant day into the answer.

RAINER MARIA RILKE, *LETTERS TO A YOUNG POET*

"How many loaves of bread do you have?" (Mark 6:38)

Before You Begin

Take some time to reflect and prepare your heart and mind for this study. Read the following Scripture passage. Soak up God's Word. There's no hurry. Then, when you're ready, turn the page and begin.

JEREMIAH 1:5-8

"Before I shaped you in the womb,
  I knew all about you.
Before you saw the light of day,
  I had holy plans for you:
A prophet to the nations—
  that's what I had in mind for you."

But I said, "Hold it, Master GOD! Look at me.
  I don't know anything. I'm only a boy!"

GOD told me, "Don't say, 'I'm only a boy.'
  I'll tell you where to go and you'll go there.
I'll tell you what to say and you'll say it.
  Don't be afraid of a soul.
I'll be right there, looking after you."

READ

Mark 6:30-44

The apostles then rendezvoused with Jesus and reported on all that they had done and taught. Jesus said, "Come off by yourselves; let's take a break and get a little rest." For there was constant coming and going. They didn't even have time to eat.

So they got in the boat and went off to a remote place by themselves. Someone saw them going and the word got around. From the surrounding towns people went out on foot, running, and got there ahead of them. When Jesus arrived, he saw this huge crowd. At the sight of them, his heart broke—like sheep with no shepherd they were. He went right to work teaching them.

When his disciples thought this had gone on long enough—it was now quite late in the day—they interrupted: "We are a long way out in the country, and it's very late. Pronounce a benediction and send these folks off so they can get some supper."

Jesus said, "You do it. Fix supper for them."

They replied, "Are you serious? You want us to go spend a fortune on food for their supper?"

But he was quite serious. **"How many loaves of bread do you have?** Take an inventory."

That didn't take long. "Five," they said, "plus two fish."

Jesus got them all to sit down in groups of fifty or a hundred—they looked like a patchwork quilt of wildflowers spread out on the green grass! He took the five loaves and two fish, lifted his face to heaven in prayer, blessed, broke, and gave the bread to the disciples, and the disciples in turn gave it to the people. He did the same with the fish. They all ate their fill. The disciples gathered twelve baskets of leftovers. More than five thousand were at the supper.

THINK   "How many loaves of bread do you have?"

- What is your immediate response to this question?
- Why do you think you responded in this way?
- Do you believe this really happened, or is this just a figurative story? Why do you think this way?
- What are your thoughts about the disciples in the first half of the story?
- Think about the obstacles the disciples saw in this situation: distance ("a long way out in the country"), time ("it's very late"), and numbers ("this huge crowd"). Notice that though the disciples saw problems, Jesus saw people ("At the sight of them, his heart broke"). What does this tell you about the disciples? About Jesus?

READ

From *Letters to a Young Poet*, by Rainer Maria Rilke[1]

> Then try, like some first human being, to say what you see and experience and love and lose. . . . Describe your sorrows and desires, passing thoughts and the belief in some sort of beauty—describe all these with loving, quiet, humble sincerity, and use, to express yourself, the things in your environment, the images from your dreams, and the objects of your memory. If your daily life seems poor, do not blame it; blame yourself, tell yourself that you are not poet enough to call forth its riches; for to the creator there is no poverty and no poor indifferent place. And even if you were in some prison the walls of which let none of the sounds of the world come to your senses—would you not then still have your childhood, that precious, kingly possession, that treasure-house of memories?

THINK   "How many loaves of bread do you have?"

- Think about a time when you were overwhelmed in a situation and couldn't see a way out. Describe that time in as much detail as possible.
- The question Jesus asked is essentially, "Well, what have you got? What do you have that's here right now?" Look back into the situation you just described for anything that could have been useful. Look for something God could have used that you overlooked. Take your time.
- Consider accepting the challenge to become one of God's poets—one who is courageous enough to call forth the riches in any given situation, one who knows that with Jesus in the room, "there is no poverty and no poor indifferent place." How might you go about this?

THINK (continued)

READ

From *Community and Growth*, by Jean Vanier[2]

> Some people, who cannot see what nourishment they could be bringing, do not realize that they can become bread for others. They have no confidence that their word, their smile, their being, or their prayer could nourish others and help them rediscover trust. Jesus calls us to give our lives for those we love. If we eat the bread transformed into the Body of Christ, it is so that we become bread for others.
>
> Others find their own nourishment is to give from an empty basket! It is the miracle of the multiplication of the bread. "Lord, let me seek not so much to be consoled as to console." I am always astonished to discover that I can give a nourishing talk when I feel empty, and that I can still transmit peace when I feel anguished. Only God can perform that sort of miracle.

THINK   "How many loaves of bread do you have?"

- What do you think of Vanier's thoughts?
- Do you often think of yourself as "bread for others"? If you do, describe a time when you nourished someone. If you don't, try to think through why that concept is so foreign to you.
- How about the "empty basket" experience Vanier talks about? Have you ever given out of your emptiness, only to have God multiply?

READ

From *Crossing the Unknown Sea*, by David Whyte[3]

To have faith in the night means that we have a secret loyalty to things other than those that are so slavishly celebrated by all the others in the day. In the surface conversation of our colleague we listen for the undercurrent; the persistent tug and ebb that tells us she is actually going in the opposite direction to her speech. Beneath the surface of our morning commute we realize that something is taking us away in the opposite direction, that wants not just another job but another life. Watching the newscast, we realize this news is no news at all but someone else's priorities centered mostly in extremely perverse ways on the NASDAQ and the Dow Jones. A friendship with the night means we are impatient with propaganda, manipulation, advertising, the overilluminated and over-stated. We become immensely tired of hearing, from those who have no time in their own lives to stop and think deeply, that this is the *age of information.*

"Loaves and Fishes," by David Whyte[4]

This is not
the age of information.

This is *not*
the age of information.

Forget the news,
and the radio,
and the blurred screen.

This is the time
of loaves
and fishes.

People are hungry,
and one good word is bread
for a thousand.

THINK "How many loaves of bread do you have?"

- How do Whyte's words, especially his poem, strike you?
- Whyte invites us to think about the situations we usually find ourselves in, those situations in which information seems to be what is needed. He says that information is not what we need, but that "people are hungry, and one good word is bread for a thousand." Do you agree with him? Why or why not?
- To get to those good words, we must "have a secret loyalty to things other than those that are so slavishly celebrated by all the others in the day." Think about this: The disciples saw it was getting late and immediately thought of eating, something "slavishly celebrated" by most people. However, there was something else going on there: good words! Do you think it's possible the people would have stayed and listened and never thought about food had the disciples not shown the focus of their loyalty?
- What truths about your own life can you extract from this story?

PRAY

Look back at the "Think" sections. Ruminate on your responses. Let them distill into a prayer, and then write that prayer below.

Bread of Life . . .

The issue of prayer is not prayer; the issue of prayer is God.

ABRAHAM HESCHEL

LIVE

"How many loaves of bread do you have?"

The challenge now is to take this question further along—to live out
this question. Think of one thing, *just one*, that you can personally do
to wrestle with the question, inhabit the character of it, and live it in
everyday life. In the following space, jot down your thoughts on this
"one thing." Read the Scripture and quotes that follow for additional
inspiration. During the coming week, pray about this "one thing," talk
with a close friend about it, and learn to live the question.

One thing . . .

Do not look back. And do not dream about the future, either.
It will neither give you back the past, nor satisfy your other
  daydreams.
Your duty, your reward—your destiny—are *here* and *now*.
Dag Hammarskjold

"The simple truth is that if you had a mere kernel of faith, a
poppy seed, say, you would tell this mountain, 'Move!' and
it would move. There is nothing you wouldn't be able to
tackle."

Matthew 17:20

Live the questions now. Perhaps you will then gradually, without
noticing it, live along some distant day into the answer.
RAINER MARIA RILKE, *LETTERS TO A YOUNG POET*

"Don't you see that what you swallow
can't contaminate you?" (Mark 7:18)

Before You Begin

Take some time to reflect and prepare your heart and mind
for this study. Read the following Scripture passage. Soak
up God's Word. There's no hurry. Then, when you're ready,
turn the page and begin.

Isaiah 29:13-14

The Master said:

"These people make a big show of saying the right thing,
  but their hearts aren't in it.
Because they act like they're worshiping me
  but don't mean it,
I'm going to step in and shock them awake,
  astonish them, stand them on their ears.
The wise ones who had it all figured out
  will be exposed as fools.
The smart people who thought they knew everything
  will turn out to know nothing."

READ

Mark 7:1-23

The Pharisees, along with some religion scholars who had come from Jerusalem, gathered around him. They noticed that some of his disciples weren't being careful with ritual washings before meals. The Pharisees—Jews in general, in fact—would never eat a meal without going through the motions of a ritual hand-washing, with an especially vigorous scrubbing if they had just come from the market (to say nothing of the scourings they'd give jugs and pots and pans).

The Pharisees and religion scholars asked, "Why do your disciples flout the rules, showing up at meals without washing their hands?"

Jesus answered, "Isaiah was right about frauds like you, hit the bull's-eye in fact:

These people make a big show of saying the right thing,
> but their heart isn't in it.
They act like they are worshiping me,
> but they don't mean it.
They just use me as a cover
> for teaching whatever suits their fancy,
Ditching God's command
> and taking up the latest fads."

He went on, "Well, good for you. You get rid of God's command so you won't be inconvenienced in following the religious fashions! Moses said, 'Respect your father and mother,' and, 'Anyone denouncing father or mother should be killed.' But you weasel out of that by saying that it's perfectly acceptable to say to father or mother, 'Gift! What I owed you I've given as a gift to God,' thus relieving yourselves of obligation to father or mother. You scratch out God's Word and scrawl a whim in its place. You do a lot of things like this."

Jesus called the crowd together again and said, "Listen now, all of you—take this to heart. It's not what you swallow that pollutes your life; it's what you vomit—that's the real pollution."

When he was back home after being with the crowd, his disciples said, "We don't get it. Put it in plain language."

Jesus said, "Are you being willfully stupid? **Don't you see that what you swallow can't contaminate you?** It doesn't enter your heart but your stomach, works its way through the intestines, and is finally flushed." (That took care of dietary quibbling; Jesus was saying that *all* foods are fit to eat.)

He went on: "It's what comes out of a person that pollutes: obscenities, lusts, thefts, murders, adulteries, greed, depravity, deceptive dealings, carousing, mean looks, slander, arrogance, foolishness—all these are vomit from the heart. *There* is the source of your pollution."

THINK   "Don't you see that what you swallow can't contaminate you?"

- What is your immediate response to this question?
- Why do you think you responded in this way?
- Write down your impressions from this passage.
- Can you come up with a couple of "rules" from your religious experience that would parallel the ritual hand-washing of the Pharisees?
- What is your reaction to the phrase "vomit from the heart"?

READ

From *New Seeds of Contemplation*, by Thomas Merton[1]

Some men seem to think that a saint cannot possibly take a natural interest in anything created. They imagine that any form of spontaneity or enjoyment is a sinful gratification of "fallen nature." That to be "supernatural" means obstructing all spontaneity with clichés and arbitrary references to God. The purpose of these clichés is, so to speak, to hold everything at arm's length, to frustrate spontaneous reactions, to exorcise feelings of guilt. Or perhaps to cultivate such feelings! One wonders sometimes if such morality is not after all a love of guilt! They suppose that the life of a saint can never be anything but a perpetual duel with guilt, and that a saint cannot even drink a glass of cold water without making an act of contrition for slaking his thirst, as if that were a mortal sin. As if for the saints every response to beauty, to goodness, to the pleasant, were an offense. As if the saint could never allow himself to be pleased with anything but his prayers and his interior acts of piety.

THINK   "Don't you see that what you swallow can't contaminate you?"

- Are you someone who thinks "a saint cannot possibly take a natural interest in anything created"? Why do you think that way? (And don't forget, we're all considered saints when we enter into a relationship with Christ.)
- Do you know anyone who obstructs "all spontaneity with clichés and arbitrary references to God"? How do you relate to this person?
- Have you ever believed that your life of faith might require you to avoid all things that seem unspiritual?
- Consider this quote: "One wonders sometimes if such morality is not after all a love of guilt!" Do you agree or disagree with this statement? Why?

THINK (continued)

READ

From *The Post-Evangelical*, by Dave Tomlinson[2]

> My contention is that middle-class values form the dominant cultural norm in most evangelical churches, and these values function in a similar way judaizing did in the early church, by which I mean that they impregnate the very nature of the gospel. . . . This in itself is no bad thing, representing as it does a perfectly valid point of view. There are two problems about it which I will mention. The first is that it is generally accompanied by an upward materialistic spiral. In his challenging book *A Long Way from Home* Tony Walter says that Christians have tended to move up the social scale and gradually surrounded themselves with the trappings of a suburban lifestyle. . . .
>
> But the more significant problem, from the point of view of our present discussion, is that middle-class evangelicals (and they are not alone in this) create what Walter refers to as "culture religion," that is, they identify Christianity with the standards, values and attitudes of their own culture: in this case, middle-class culture:
>
>> Christians may not be aware of the extent to which they have conformed to a middle-class lifestyle. So many of the public values of a society are middle-class that these values, which are far from inevitable or God-given, are taken for granted. Some Christians, because they have one or two taboos such as not drinking or swearing which set them apart from other people, are able to convince themselves that they are not conforming to society. By focusing their attention on gambling or drink, they ignore the way in which they have unconsciously absorbed their neighbor's views on virtually everything else. They strain at a gnat and swallow a whole cultural mule.
>
> The real issue is: in what ways are we supposed to be different from the rest of the world? We must return again and again to the wise conclusion of the early apostles: that believers should not be

saddled with greater burdens than is absolutely necessary. Rather than perpetuating religious taboos, we need to decide what is really necessary and then leave the rest for people to decide for themselves. Tony Campolo reminds us of our true priorities:

> Both U.S. and U.K. evangelicalism have defined a Christian as someone more pious than the rest of the world. Personally, piety turns me off! The Christian is radically compassionate, not pious. What did people say about Jesus? They didn't call him pious! He had a lousy testimony. Did anybody ever call him spiritual? They called him winebibber, glutton, someone who hangs around with whores and publicans. Jesus was too busy expressing compassion to measure up to the expectations of piety. And I think we need to be more Christ-like.

THINK   *"Don't you see that what you swallow can't contaminate you?"*

- What is your reaction to Tomlinson's words?
- Did he say anything that made you bristle? If so, what?
- Tomlinson says, "Rather than perpetuating religious taboos, we need to decide what is really necessary and then leave the rest for people to decide for themselves." Do you agree or disagree with this statement? Why?
- Define *piety* in your own words. What do you think of Campolo's disgust with it? What is your opinion of it?

READ

An example of "vomit from the heart" that Jesus talked about in the passage from Mark is the rejection of the obligation to take care of one's father and mother. We'll end this lesson by turning the question in that direction. Created things (Merton) or non-middle-class values (Tomlinson) cannot contaminate you, but a lack of compassion toward your parents surely can. Here is a reading from Walter Wangerin Jr. that speaks to this.

From *Little Lamb, Who Made Thee?*, by Walter Wangerin Jr.[3]

The commandments have not expired. Nor have the holy promises that attend them been abolished.

When, therefore, I am asked regarding the future of some human community, some family, some nation—or the church, the visible church itself!—straightway I look for obedience to the commandments of God. Particularly I wonder regarding the one which urges honor for the parents: I look to see whether someone is singing songs to his aged mother—and if I can find him, I say, "The signs are good."

This is no joke. The best prognostication for the life of any community—whether it shall be long or short—is not financial, political, demographic, or even theological. It is moral. Ask not, "How strong is the nation?" nor "How many are they? How well organized? With what armies and resources?" Ask, rather: *How does this people behave?*

See, there is always set before us life and good or death and evil. If we walk in the ways of the sustaining God and obey his commandments, then we have chosen life—for the Lord is life and the length of any nation's days. This is flat practicality. How we are defines whether we shall continue to be.

Do we as a people honor our mothers and fathers? Do we honor the generation that raised us—especially when it sinks down into an old and seemingly dishonorable age? When our parents twist and bow and begin to stink, what then? When they harden in crankiness, what then? Do we by esteeming them make them sweet and lovely again? The question is not irrelevant to our future, whether we shall have one or not. Its answer verily prophesies of *That it may be well with you and you may live long on the earth.*

The Hebrew word here translated earth may also be translated land, meaning more than just soil, meaning country. The promise attached to this commandment is precise: so long as the Israelites honored their parents, they would continue to live in the land that God had provided for them. If ever they began to neglect their parents or, worse, to scorn or in some way to hurt them, that break between the generations would break the people from their land as a sick tree breaks at the trunk and dies.

Even so we—as long as we sing to the mother who bore us the songs she heard in her youth, the same songs once she sang to us in lullaby—we may live long in the land. . . .

[What follows is a short description of one of Wangerin's friends.]

M. himself was crouched at her bedside with a pan of water and cloths. He turned and saw me in the doorway. He smiled and motioned me to sit. I sat in his chair, under his reading lamp, granting them the privacy of darkness—but by the odor in the room I know what my friend was doing.

He was honoring his mother, exactly as the Lord God commanded.

He was washing away the waste. He was changing her diapers. And he was singing to her.

Softly, in his mother's tongue, he was singing *Mude bin ich, geh zu ruh*—Lullabies. The simple, sacred, everlasting songs.

And she was singing with him. That was the sound I had been hearing: no lamentation, no hurt or sorrow, but an elderly woman singing with outrageous pleasure at the top of her lungs.

And lo: This old face was alive again. This old woman was as young as the child who first heard the lullaby, innocent, happy, wholly consoled. This old mother of my friend was dwelling in the music of her childhood. This was the face of one beloved, whose son obeyed the covenant and honored her—and kept her honorable thereby.

This boisterous singer is my sign. And the sign is good. Shall we endure? So long as such obedience continues among us, O my people, yes, it may be well with us. We may live long on the earth.

THINK   *"Don't you see that what you swallow can't contaminate you?"*

- What are some of your responses to this passage?
- Do you agree or disagree with the author's thoughts? Why?
- Think for a while about your parents. Maybe they were good, bad, ugly, or some combination of the three. What do you recall of their connection with *their* parents in old age? Were they present, absent, occasional, something else? Were your grandparents honored?
- What about you? If your parents are still living, are they being honored by you? If so, how?
- If they're not being honored by you, do you have the courage to look for at least one "source of your pollution"? What might a cleanup look like?

PRAY

Look back at the "Think" sections. Ruminate on your responses.
Let them distill into a prayer, and then write that prayer below.

Give us clean hands, give us clean hearts . . .

The issue of prayer is not prayer; the issue of prayer is God.

ABRAHAM HESCHEL

LIVE

"Don't you see that what you swallow can't contaminate you?"

The challenge now is to take this question further along—to live out this question. Think of one thing, *just one*, that you can personally do to wrestle with the question, inhabit the character of it, and live it in everyday life. In the following space, jot down your thoughts on this "one thing." Read the Scripture and quotes that follow for additional inspiration. During the coming week, pray about this "one thing," talk with a close friend about it, and learn to live the question.

One thing . . .

Honor your father and mother so that you'll live a long time in the land that GOD, your God, is giving you.

Exodus 20:12

Life is complicated and not for the timid. It's an experience that when it's done, it will take us a while to get over it. We'll look back on all the good things we surrendered in favor of deadly trash and wish we had returned and reclaimed them.

Garrison Keillor

Live the questions now. Perhaps you will then gradually, without noticing it, live along some distant day into the answer.

RAINER MARIA RILKE, *LETTERS TO A YOUNG POET*

"Why does this generation clamor for
miraculous guarantees?" (Mark 8:12)

Before You Begin

Take some time to reflect and prepare your heart and mind
for this study. Read the following Scripture passage. Soak
up God's Word. There's no hurry. Then, when you're ready,
turn the page and begin.

Hebrews 11:1-3

The fundamental fact of existence is that this trust in God,
this faith, is the firm foundation under everything that
makes life worth living. It's our handle on what we can't see.
The act of faith is what distinguished our ancestors, set them
above the crowd.

By faith, we see the world called into existence by God's
word, what we see created by what we don't see.

READ

Mark 8:1-15

At about this same time he again found himself with a hungry crowd on his hands. He called his disciples together and said, "This crowd is breaking my heart. They have stuck with me for three days, and now they have nothing to eat. If I send them home hungry, they'll faint along the way—some of them have come a long distance."

His disciples responded, "What do you expect us to do about it? Buy food out here in the desert?"

He asked, "How much bread do you have?"

"Seven loaves," they said.

So Jesus told the crowd to sit down on the ground. After giving thanks, he took the seven bread loaves, broke them into pieces, and gave them to his disciples so they could hand them out to the crowd. They also had a few fish. He pronounced a blessing over the fish and told his disciples to hand them out as well. The crowd ate its fill. Seven sacks of leftovers were collected. There were well over four thousand at the meal. Then he sent them home. He himself went straight to the boat with his disciples and set out for Dalmanoutha.

When they arrived, the Pharisees came out and started in on him, badgering him to prove himself, pushing him up against the wall. Provoked, he said, "**Why does this generation clamor for miraculous guarantees?** If I have anything to say about it, you'll not get so much as a hint of a guarantee."

He then left them, got back in the boat, and headed for the other side. But the disciples forgot to pack a lunch. Except for a single loaf of bread, there wasn't a crumb in the boat. Jesus warned, "Be very careful. Keep a sharp eye out for the contaminating yeast of Pharisees and the followers of Herod."

THINK "Why does this generation clamor for miraculous guarantees?"

- What is your immediate response to this question?
- Why do you think you responded in this way?
- Give your best definition of faith. Try to avoid sounding like a Scripture verse or a church slogan.
- The two major groups in this passage are the disciples and the Pharisees. Evaluate them based on your definition of faith. Are they faithful or faithless? Explain why you answered the way you did.

READ

From *The Orphean Passages*, by Walter Wangerin Jr.[1]

Ah, little children! Faith is not yet surcease, nor hiding, nor retreat, nor an island in the waters. Ah, children, you cheapen it by your chatter, judging some to be "in faith" and others "out of faith" as though it were a fixed condition and you, the "faithful" had the right to make the distinctions, as though faith, once experienced, were ever thereafter the same. Oh, dear children, "faithing" is neither a stone nor doctrine nor any product of your desiring. It is, rather, the frightful thing: a *drama*, wherein God is the protagonist, the first and greater wrestler, while we are the antagonist, Jacob at Peniel, terribly, terribly deep in the night.

And having said so, I commiserate with you. It is hard, indeed.

For such dark drama as this *does* dissolve our power over anything. No, we cannot keep a thing, not even ourselves nor our identities; and it does insist that something else has power over us, even a thing we cannot fully know nor name (though faithing is finally the process of namings, his and ours together). And so we are afraid, dear children. I know. And sometimes we feel so lost.

Faith, if ever it is to be a noun, is properly the whole play, from the first scene to the last, done up and done. But we do not know the last until we are there, until we have come to it both through and by our tribulation. (God knows; but we don't know as we are known.) Therefore, while we are still involved in it, we cannot truly use the fixing noun. "Faithing" allows—appallingly, it presumes—change.

But having heard that, hear too the blessing it implies:

When the relationship between the Lord and us is troubled; when we, like Jeremiah, spit against the Deity; or when we cry, as surely we will in the deep sincerity of our souls, "There is no God!" then, if all we had for definition were the noun *faith*, we would have to judge ourselves faith-less, fallen from the faith, cast out. And that were the worst of deaths to die. On the other hand, if it is faithing which we are experiencing, and if this desolated cry arises from one scene in a long and fluid play, then even the desolation may have its place in the changing relationship, caused by previous action, causing actions subsequent; then despair may be an episode in the drama. And then we are not fallen from the faith, but rather falling within it—and even this, dear child, may be *of* the faith.

For faithing consists in the living relationship. And the whole of the actor's involved: his soul and his body, his eyes and all he sees, his cowlick, his mouth, his ecstasies and his dejections. And when he dies not isolate, but dies from scene to scene, from gesture to gesture, and horror to holiness, why, that were a fruitful death indeed.

THINK "Why does this generation clamor for miraculous guarantees?"

- What impressions do Wangerin's words have on you?
- Think about a time when someone you know, or possibly you yourself, was judged to be "out of the faith." What was behind the judgment? Be specific. Who made the judgment?
- Wangerin says that faith is the drama, not the fixed condition. How do you feel about that distinction?
- How does that line up with your previous definition of faith?

READ

From *Teaching a Stone to Talk*, by Annie Dillard[2]

You have seen photographs of the sun taken during a total eclipse. The corona fills the print. All of those photographs were taken through telescopes. The lenses of telescopes and cameras can no more cover the breadth and scale of the visual array than language can cover the breadth and simultaneity of internal experience. Lenses enlarge the sight, omit its context, and make of it a pretty and sensible picture, like something on a Christmas card. I assure you, if you send any shepherds a Christmas card on which is printed a three-by-three photograph of the angel of the Lord, the glory of the Lord, and a multitude of the heavenly host, they will not be sore afraid.

THINK   "Why does this generation clamor for miraculous guarantees?"

- How does a miraculous guarantee operate like a telescope or camera?
- What vista does faith require in order to be fully realized? How does the demand for miracles or guarantees shrink that vista?
- Why do you think our generation clamors for fixed, photographic images; tips; techniques; and miraculous guarantees?
- Re-read this sentence: "The lenses of telescopes and cameras can no more cover the breadth and scale of the visual array than language can cover the breadth and simultaneity of internal experience." How does this speak to your experience of faith?

READ

From *The Jesus I Never Knew*, by Philip Yancey[3]

The feeding . . . illustrates why Jesus, with all the supernatural powers at his command, showed such an ambivalence toward miracles. They attracted crowds and applause, yes, but rarely encouraged repentance and long-term faith. He was bringing a hard message of obedience and sacrifice, not a sideshow for gawkers and sensation-seekers.

From that day on, Jesus' teaching had a different twist. As if the back-to-back scenes of acclamation and rejection had clarified his future, he began to talk much more openly about his death. The odd figures of speech he had used against the crowd began to make more sense. The bread of life was not magic, like manna; it came down from heaven in order to be broken, and mixed with blood. He was talking about his own body. In the words of Robert Farrar Capon, "the Messiah was not going to save the world by miraculous, Band-Aid interventions: a storm calmed here, a crowd fed there, a mother-in-law cured back down the road. Rather, it was going to be saved by means of a deeper, darker, left-handed mystery, at the center of which lay his own death."

"A wicked and adulterous generation asks for a miraculous sign!" Jesus would say when someone else asked for a display of his powers. And in Jerusalem, the capital, though many people saw the miracles he did and believed in him, "he would not entrust himself to them," for he knew what was in their hearts.

A sign is not the same thing as proof; a sign is merely a marker for someone who is looking in the right direction.

THINK   "Why does this generation clamor for miraculous guarantees?"

- What thoughts do Yancey's words evoke in you?
- Which of the following best describes our current generation: people of obedience and sacrifice or "gawkers and sensation-seekers"? Which best describes most churches? Most individual believers? You?
- Based on all you've read and thought about in this lesson, offer your best definition of faith again.

PRAY

Look back at the "Think" sections. Ruminate on your responses. Let them distill into a prayer, and then write that prayer below.

First and greater Wrestler . . .

The issue of prayer is not prayer; the issue of prayer is God.

ABRAHAM HESCHEL

LIVE   "Why does this generation clamor for miraculous guarantees?"

The challenge now is to take this question further along—to live out this question. Think of one thing, *just one*, that you can personally do to wrestle with the question, inhabit the character of it, and live it in everyday life. In the following space, jot down your thoughts on this "one thing." Read the quotes that follow for additional inspiration. During the coming week, pray about this "one thing," talk with a close friend about it, and learn to live the question.

One thing . . .

But enough is enough. One turns at least even from glory itself with a sigh of relief. From the depths of mystery, and even from the heights of splendor, we bounce back and hurry for the latitudes of home.

Annie Dillard

The important point to make about the proofs is that even at their convincing best, they just wing God on the earlobe, as it were. They don't tell you much.

Robert Farrar Capon

Live the questions now. Perhaps you will then gradually, without noticing it, live along some distant day into the answer.

RAINER MARIA RILKE, *LETTERS TO A YOUNG POET*

"Who do the people say I am?" (Mark 8:27)

Before You Begin

Take some time to reflect and prepare your heart and mind for this study. Read the following Scripture passage. Soak up God's Word. There's no hurry. Then, when you're ready, turn the page and begin.

Isaiah 53:1-3

Who believes what we've heard and seen?
Who would have thought God's saving power would
    look like this?

The servant grew up before God—a scrawny seedling,
    a scrubby plant in a parched field.
There was nothing attractive about him,
    nothing to cause us to take a second look.
He was looked down on and passed over,
    a man who suffered, who knew pain firsthand.
One look at him and people turned away.
    We looked down on him, thought he was scum.

READ

Mark 8:27-38

Jesus and his disciples headed out for the villages around Caesarea Philippi. As they walked, he asked, **"Who do the people say I am?"**

"Some say 'John the Baptizer,'" they said. "Others say, 'Elijah.' Still others say 'one of the prophets.'"

He then asked, "And you—what are you saying about me? Who am I?"

Peter gave the answer: "You are the Christ, the Messiah."

Jesus warned them to keep it quiet, not to breathe a word of it to anyone. He then began explaining things to them: "It is necessary that the Son of Man proceed to an ordeal of suffering, be tried and found guilty by the elders, high priests, and religion scholars, be killed, and after three days rise up alive." He said this simply and clearly so they couldn't miss it.

But Peter grabbed him in protest. Turning and seeing his disciples wavering, wondering what to believe, Jesus confronted Peter. "Peter, get out of my way! Satan, get lost! You have no idea how God works."

Calling the crowd to join his disciples, he said, "Anyone who intends to come with me has to let me lead. You're not in the driver's seat; *I* am. Don't run from suffering; embrace it. Follow me and I'll show you how. Self-help is no help at all. Self-sacrifice is the way, my way, to saving yourself, your true self. What good would it do to get everything you want and lose you, the real you? What could you ever trade your soul for?

"If any of you are embarrassed over me and the way I'm leading you when you get around your fickle and unfocused friends, know that you'll be an even greater embarrassment to the Son of Man when he arrives in all the splendor of God, his Father, with an army of the holy angels."

THINK   "Who do the people say I am?"

- What is your immediate response to this question?
- Why do you think you responded in this way?
- What are some things that strike you about this passage?
- Jesus' question points to the heart of this idea of identity. Why do you think that's key?
- How do you feel about the fact that Peter gave the definitive answer?
- What do the names *Christ* and *Messiah* mean to you?

(God among us

READ

From *The Challenge of Jesus*, by N. T. Wright[1]

I believe, in fact, that the historical quest for Jesus is a necessary and nonnegotiable aspect of Christian discipleship and that we in our generation have a chance to be renewed in discipleship and mission precisely by means of this quest. I want to explain and justify these beliefs from the outset. There are, however, huge problems and even dangers within the quest, as one would expect from anything that is heavy with potential for the Kingdom of God, and I shall need to say something about these as well.

There are well-known pitfalls in even addressing the subject, and we may as well be clear about them. It is desperately easy when among like-minded friends to become complacent. We hear of wild new theories about Jesus. Every month or two some publisher comes up with a blockbuster saying that he was a New Age guru, an Egyptian freemason or a hippie revolutionary. Every year or two some scholar or group of scholars comes up with a new book full of imposing footnotes to tell us that Jesus was a peasant Cynic, a wandering wordsmith or the preacher of liberal values born out of due time.

The day I was redrafting this chapter for publication, a newspaper article appeared about a new controversy, initiated by animal-rights activists, as to whether Jesus was a vegetarian.

We may well react to this sort of thing by saying that it is all a waste of time, that we know all we need to know about Jesus, and there is no more to be said. Many devout Christians taking this line content themselves with an effortless superiority: we know the truth, these silly liberals have got it all wrong, and we have nothing new to learn. Sometimes people like me are wheeled out to demonstrate, supposedly, the truth of "traditional Christianity," with the implied corollary that we can now stop asking these unpleasant historical questions and get on with something else, perhaps something more profitable, instead.

Some, however, react by reaching for equally misleading alternative stereotypes. A defense of a would-be "supernatural" Jesus can easily degenerate into a portrayal of Jesus as a first-century version of Superman—not realizing that the Superman myth is itself ultimately a dualistic corruption of the Christian story. There are several Jesus pictures on offer that appear very devout but that ignore what the New Testament actually says about the human being Jesus of Nazareth or what it means in its original context.

I do not intend to encourage any of these attitudes. . . . But since orthodox Christianity has always held firm to the basic belief that it is by looking at Jesus himself that we discover who God is, it seems to me indisputable that we should expect always to be continuing in the quest for Jesus precisely as part of, indeed perhaps as the sharp edge of, our exploration into God himself.

THINK "Who do the people say I am?"

- Who do the people today say Jesus is? Think about the people you know: friends, family members, work associates.
- Do you agree with this statement: "I believe, in fact, that the historical quest for Jesus is a necessary and nonnegotiable aspect of Christian discipleship and that we in our generation have a chance to be renewed in discipleship and mission precisely by means of this quest"? Why or why not?
- Think about those who have been formative in your faith: teachers, pastors, parents, friends. How would they react to the idea that "we know all we need to know about Jesus, and there is no more to be said"? What's your reaction to it? Why?

READ

From *God in the Dock*, by C. S. Lewis[2]

What are we to make of Jesus Christ? This is a question which has, in a sense, a frantically comic side. For the real question is not what are we to make of Christ, but what is He to make of us? The picture of a fly sitting deciding what it is going to make of an elephant has comic elements about it. But perhaps the questioner meant what are we to make of Him in the sense of 'How are we to solve the historical problem set us by the recorded sayings and acts of this Man?' This problem is to reconcile two things. On the one hand you have got the almost generally admitted depth and sanity of His moral teaching, which is not very seriously questioned, even by those who are opposed to Christianity. In fact, I find when I am arguing with very anti-God people that they rather make a point of saying, 'I am entirely in favour of the moral teaching of Christianity'—and there seems to be a general agreement that in the teaching of this Man and of His immediate followers, moral truth is exhibited at its purest and best. It is not sloppy idealism, it is full of wisdom and shrewdness. The whole thing is realistic, fresh to the highest degree, the product of a sane mind. That is one phenomenon.

From *God in the Dock*, by C. S. Lewis[3]

The idea of a great moral teacher saying what Christ said is out of the question. In my opinion, the only person who can say that sort of thing is either God or a complete lunatic suffering from that form of delusion which undermines the whole mind of man. If you think you are a poached egg, when you are looking for a piece of toast to suit you, you may be sane, but if you think you are God, there is no chance for you. We may note in passing that He was never regarded as a mere moral teacher. He did not produce that effect on any of the people who actually met Him. He produced mainly three effects—Hatred—Terror—Adoration. There was no trace of people expressing mild approval.

THINK   "Who do the people say I am?"

- What words or phrases made an impression on you from this passage?
- Do most people you know have any problem with the moral teachings of Jesus? Explain.
- Think about these words from Lewis: "We may note in passing that He was never regarded as a mere moral teacher. He did not produce that effect on any of the people who actually met Him. He produced mainly three effects—Hatred—Terror—Adoration. There was no trace of people expressing mild approval." Write down your initial reaction. Then read the words a few more times, resting in the depth of their meaning. Note any discoveries you have as you wrestle with Lewis's ideas.

READ

From *Orthodoxy*, by G. K. Chesterton[4]

Instead of looking at books and pictures about the New Testament I looked at the New Testament. There I found an account, not in the least of a person with his hair parted in the middle or his hands clasped in appeal, but of an extraordinary being with lips of thunder and acts of lurid decision, flinging down tables, casting out devils, passing with the wild secrecy of the wind from mountain isolation to a sort of dreadful demagogy; a being who often acted like an angry god—and always like a god. Christ had even a literary style of his own, not to be found, I think, elsewhere; it consists of an almost furious use of the *a fortiori*. His "how much more" is piled one upon another like castle upon castle in the clouds. The diction used *about* Christ has been, and perhaps wisely, sweet and submissive. But the diction used by Christ is quite curiously gigantesque; it is full of camels leaping through needles and mountains hurled into the sea. Morally it is equally terrific; he called himself a sword of slaughter, and told men to buy swords if they sold their coats for them. That he used other even wilder words on the side of non-resistance greatly increases the mystery; but it also, if anything, rather increases the violence. We cannot even explain it by calling such a being insane; for insanity is usually along one consistent channel. The maniac is generally a monomaniac. Here we must remember the difficult definition of Christianity already given; Christianity is a superhuman paradox whereby two opposite passions may blaze beside each other.

THINK   "Who do the people say I am?"

- Think about this: Although the first question in this passage from Mark is "Who do the people say I am?" the follow-up question for the disciples is, "And you—what are you saying about me? Who am I?" It becomes very personal, as it should.

- From where have *you* drawn your impressions regarding Christ? From books and pictures about the New Testament or from the New Testament itself? From the experience of others or from your own experiences?

- Based on your answer to the previous question, who do *you* say Jesus is? What does your answer reveal about you? About your relationship with him?

PRAY

Look back at the "Think" sections. Ruminate on your responses. Let them distill into a prayer, and then write that prayer below.

You are the Christ, the Messiah . . . Who is an exemplary role model to those who will follow We pray more will listen & many more will follow. Be with us & comfort us particularly in rough times as we seek to be better Christians —

The issue of prayer is not prayer; the issue of prayer is God.

ABRAHAM HESCHEL

LIVE   "Who do the people say I am?"

The challenge now is to take this question further along—to live out this question. Think of one thing, *just one*, that you can personally do to wrestle with the question, inhabit the character of it, and live it in everyday life. In the following space, jot down your thoughts on this "one thing." Read the quotes that follow for additional inspiration. During the coming week, pray about this "one thing," talk with a close friend about it, and learn to live the question.

One thing . . .

He was not at all like the psychologist's picture of the integrated, balanced, adjusted, happily married, employed, popular citizen. You can't really be very well "adjusted" to your world if it says you "have a devil" and ends up nailing you naked to a stake of wood.

C. S. Lewis

The other gods were strong; but Thou wast weak;
They rode, but Thou didst stumble to a throne;
But to our wounds only God's wounds can speak,
And not a god has wounds but Thou alone.

Edward Shillito

Live the questions now. Perhaps you will then gradually, without noticing it, live along some distant day into the answer.

RAINER MARIA RILKE, *LETTERS TO A YOUNG POET*

LESSON 8

"What were you discussing on the road?" (Mark 9:33)

Before You Begin

Take some time to reflect and prepare your heart and mind for this study. Read the following Scripture passage. Soak up God's Word. There's no hurry. Then, when you're ready, turn the page and begin.

JAMES 4:1-2,6

Where do you think all these appalling wars and quarrels come from? Do you think they just happen? Think again. They come about because you want your own way, and fight for it deep inside yourselves. You lust for what you don't have and are willing to kill to get it. You want what isn't yours and will risk violence to get your hands on it. . . .

It's common knowledge that "God goes against the willful proud; God gives grace to the willing humble."

READ

Mark 9:30-37

Leaving there, they went through Galilee. He didn't want anyone to know their whereabouts, for he wanted to teach his disciples. He told them, "The Son of Man is about to be betrayed to some people who want nothing to do with God. They will murder him. Three days after his murder, he will rise, alive." They didn't know what he was talking about, but were afraid to ask him about it.

They came to Capernaum. When he was safe at home, he asked them, **"What were you discussing on the road?"**

The silence was deafening—they had been arguing with one another over who among them was greatest.

He sat down and summoned the Twelve. "So you want first place? Then take the last place. Be the servant of all."

He put a child in the middle of the room. Then, cradling the little one in his arms, he said, "Whoever embraces one of these children as I do embraces me, and far more than me—God who sent me."

THINK   "What were you discussing on the road?"

- What is your immediate response to this question?
- Why do you think you responded in this way?
- Do you think Jesus knew what the disciples had been discussing? Why or why not?
- Why do you think the disciples were talking about this? Was it possibly a subject they had discussed before?
- Think about that drive in the disciples and in us that makes us desire to be the greatest. Where does that come from?
- The phrase "He sat down" tells us the teacher is about to teach. And his instruction is this: "Then take the last place. Be the servant of all." What is your reaction to these words?

THINK (continued)

READ

From *A River Runs Through It and Other Stories*, by Norman Maclean[1]

I suppose it was inevitable that my brother and I would get into one big fight which also would be the last one. When it came, given our theories about street fighting, it was like the Battle Hymn, terrible and swift. There are parts of it I did not see. I did not see our mother walk between us to try to stop us. She was short and wore glasses and, even with them on, did not have good vision. She had never seen a fight before or had any notion of how bad you can get hurt by becoming mixed up in one. Evidently, she just walked between her sons. The first I saw of her was the gray top of her head, the hair tied in a big knot with a big comb in it; but what was most noticeable was that her head was so close to Paul I couldn't get a good punch at him. Then I didn't see her anymore.

The fight seemed suddenly to stop itself. She was lying on the floor between us. Then we both began to cry and fight in a rage, each one shouting, "You . . . you knocked my mother down."

She got off the floor, and, blind without her glasses, staggered in circles between us, saying without recognizing which one she was addressing, "No, it wasn't you. I just slipped and fell."

So this was the only time we ever fought.

Perhaps we always wondered which of us was tougher, but, if boyhood questions aren't answered before a certain point in time, they can't ever be raised again. So we returned to being gracious to each other.

THINK   *"What were you discussing on the road?"*

- What impressions did this passage make on you?
- Norman's challenger in "the greatest" category was his brother, Paul. Think about your challengers over the years, as a child and as an adult. List as many as you can and the particular

fights you engaged in, literal or figurative.

• Are any of those fights still going on today?

• Think about this statement: "If boyhood questions aren't answered before a certain point in time, they can't ever be raised again." What "boyhood questions" do you continue to raise?

READ

From *Tuesdays with Morrie*, by Mitch Albom[2]

> It is 1979, a basketball game in the Brandeis gym. The team is doing well, and the student section begins a chant, "We're number one! We're number one!" Morrie is sitting nearby. He is puzzled by the cheer. At one point, in the midst of "We're number one!" he rises and yells, "What's wrong with being number two?"
>
> The students look at him. They stop chanting. He sits down, smiling and triumphant.

THINK   "What were you discussing on the road?"

- What are your reactions to this passage?
- Think about the culture in which you live (home, family, work, friends, church, and so forth). How prevalent is competition in your culture? Have you bought into it?
- How would you respond to Morrie's question, "What's wrong with being number two?"
- What would it look like to build your own subculture in which it's not just okay but actually good to be number two? How would you go about doing that?

READ

Scoreboards, by John Blase

I sat and watched a softball game last night. Actually, it was what my mother used to refer to as a "whoopin'." The home team was comprised of guys who like to get together each spring and play ball. Their ages ranged from sixteen to sixty. Most, if not all, work an eight-hour day, grab a burger and diet coke, and come straight to the games after work. They're husbands, fathers, brothers, farmers, public officials, and construction workers; the kind of men that keep the world turning. The visiting team was what is called an "industrial team." This is essentially a professional softball team that travels around the southern states throughout the spring and summer playing games and tournaments. They were young men, mostly college-aged, tan, goateed, and rippling with muscles. Goliaths in spandex. They strode to the field carrying expensive bats in expensive zip-up bags emblazoned with familiar brand names. Their girlfriends or wives followed several paces behind, respecting their "perimeters." While the home team was joking with each other, warming up and talking to the people in the stands, the visitors each had their own private rituals to enact before the game. They separated themselves from the crowd to preen and prepare.

The visitors obliterated the home team.

Their strategy? Simple. Hit one home-run after another. In the first inning alone, the visitors hit eight home runs. Eight! Hitting a home-run in softball is not an easy feat, so you get a feel for the display of strength here. Granted, the pitcher wasn't Catfish Hunter, but he knew how to pitch. While the crowd oohed and aahed at each home-run, I grew quickly weary of their exhibition. We were seeing power, raw and unleashed. This power made for a boring game. When the home team began the second inning, the flesh was willing but the spirit was gone. They no longer even paid attention to the batter, for they knew what was coming—another ooh and aah. One outfielder even began leaning on the fence, an almost vulgar stance in softball, and looked to be asleep in his cleats. Five innings were played, or endured, and the game was called. All the king's horses and all the king's men couldn't put the "home team" back together again. They had been broken.

To keep the game "alive" and involve everyone on the field, the visitors could have eased up a little and still decisively won the game. In fact, a really "hot" ground game in softball can be a hoot to watch. Everyone would have played and had fun and the right fielder wouldn't have spent so much time counting dandelions. However, on this hot, muggy, Arkansas night, the visitors had no interest in "everyone"—only themselves and their bats and their emblazoned bags.

Sometimes true skill comes not from hitting it "out" every time, but by keeping the ball "in" play. Raw power can win softball games, often after five innings. A responsible use of power can stretch a game to nine innings. Or possibly, a lifetime. The visitors took their toys and left, legends in their own minds, on to the next town. The home team returned, well, home. To trash to be taken out, children to be tucked in, news to be watched, wives to be held, and knees to be rubbed. Sometimes scoreboards lie.

THINK   "What were you discussing on the road?"

- Have you ever seen or experienced anything like this? It doesn't necessarily have to be associated with sports. Describe your impressions as you watched it play out.
- Why do you think we worship "being number one"? (The word *worship* is used intentionally because that attitude seems to be as prevalent in Christians as in non-Christians.)
- Can you recall a "number one" episode you've seen in church? How did it make you feel? Do you think the winner really won? If so, what did he or she win?

- Don't miss what's being said here. We're not talking about a lack of ambition or desire to succeed. We're talking about an attitude that keeps things "in play." Think about this question again: "What's wrong with being number two?" Or maybe number four or eight or ten?

READ

From *Where Your Treasure Is*, by Eugene H. Peterson[3]

Humility (which is the old name for unself-assertion) is probably
the least sought-after virtue in America. Mostly, it is despised. At
best it is treated with condescension, which is perhaps permis-
sible among the timorous devout who have no aptitude for the
affairs of this world. But for centuries, humility was the most
admired, if not the most practiced, of the virtues. Can so many
whom the world counted wise be wrong?

Our ancestors believed that humility was the human spirit
tempered and resilient and strong. They knew that it was difficult. They knew that even those who admired and professed
it were highly prone to subverting it in practice. John Henry
Newman is trenchant on the subject: what we usually see, he
says, is "a stooping forward unattended with the slightest effort
to leave by a single inch the seat in which we are so firmly estab-
lished. It is an act of a superior, who protests to himself while he
commits it that he is superior still, and that he is doing nothing
else but an act of grace towards those on whose level, in theory,
he is placing himself." He goes on to comment that "humility is
one of the most difficult of virtues both to attain and to ascertain.
It lies close upon the heart itself, and its tests are exceedingly
delicate and subtle. Its counterfeits abound."

But in America even the pretense to humility has been abandoned. We are led off to assertiveness-training workshops and
enrolled in management-by-objectives seminars. We are bom-
barded with techniques by which we are promised to be able
to make an impact on society. Nearly all of them turn out to be
appeals, in ways subtle or crass, to pride.

THINK   "What were you discussing on the road?"

- When was the last time you heard someone talk about humility as a virtue or saw it being practiced?
- "But in America even the pretense to humility has been abandoned." Do you agree with Peterson's statement? Why or why not?
- "Nearly all of them turn out to be appeals . . . to pride." Pride. That's what we're all "discussing on the road." And Jesus stops the discussion and speaks to it: "Then take the last place. Be the servant of all." When was the last time you took the last place? Be very specific. Did it feel great? Awkward? Forced? Right?

PRAY

Look back at the "Think" sections. Ruminate on your responses.
Let them distill into a prayer, and then write that prayer below.

God, you're Number One . . .

The issue of prayer is not prayer; the issue of prayer is God.

ABRAHAM HESCHEL

LIVE

"What were you discussing on the road?"

The challenge now is to take this question further along—to live out this question. Think of one thing, *just one*, that you can personally do to wrestle with the question, inhabit the character of it, and live it in everyday life. In the following space, jot down your thoughts on this "one thing." Read the quotes that follow for additional inspiration. During the coming week, pray about this "one thing," talk with a close friend about it, and learn to live the question.

One thing...

I am proud only of those days that pass in undivided tenderness.

Robert Bly

Violence against one is ultimately violence against all. The willingness to abuse other bodies is the willingness to abuse one's own. To damage the earth is to damage your children. To despise the ground is to despise its fruit; to despise the fruit is to despise its eaters. The wholeness of health is broken by despite.

Wendell Berry

Live the questions now. Perhaps you will then gradually, without noticing it, live along some distant day into the answer.

RAINER MARIA RILKE, *LETTERS TO A YOUNG POET*

"What do you think the owner of the vineyard will do?"

(Mark 12:9)

Before You Begin

Take some time to reflect and prepare your heart and mind
for this study. Read the following Scripture passage. Soak
up God's Word. There's no hurry. Then, when you're ready,
turn the page and begin.

JOB 42:7-8

After GOD had finished addressing Job, he turned to Eliphaz
the Temanite and said, "I've had it with you and your two
friends. I'm fed up! You haven't been honest either with
me or about me—not the way my friend Job has. So here's
what you must do. Take seven bulls and seven rams, and
go to my friend Job. Sacrifice a burnt offering on your own
behalf. My friend Job will pray for you, and I will accept his
prayer. He will ask me not to treat you as you deserve for
talking nonsense about me, and for not being honest with
me, as he has."

READ

Mark 11:27; 12:1-12

Then when they were back in Jerusalem once again, as they were walking through the Temple, the high priests, religion scholars, and leaders came up and demanded, "Show us your credentials. Who authorized you to speak and act like this?" . . .

Then Jesus started telling them stories. "A man planted a vineyard. He fenced it, dug a winepress, erected a watchtower, turned it over to the farmhands, and went off on a trip. At the time for harvest, he sent a servant back to the farmhands to collect his profits.

"They grabbed him, beat him up, and sent him off empty-handed. So he sent another servant. That one they tarred and feathered. He sent another and that one they killed. And on and on, many others. Some they beat up, some they killed.

"Finally there was only one left: a beloved son. In a last-ditch effort, he sent him, thinking, 'Surely they will respect my son.'

"But those farmhands saw their chance. They rubbed their hands together in greed and said, 'This is the heir! Let's kill him and have it all for ourselves.' They grabbed him, killed him, and threw him over the fence.

"**What do you think the owner of the vineyard will do?** Right. He'll come and clean house. Then he'll assign the care of the vineyard to others. Read it for yourselves in Scripture:

> That stone the masons threw out
>   is now the cornerstone!
> This is God's work;
>   we rub our eyes—we can hardly believe it!"

They wanted to lynch him then and there but, intimidated by public opinion, held back. They knew the story was about them. They got away from there as fast as they could.

THINK   "What do you think the owner of the vineyard will do?"

- What is your immediate response to this question?
- Why do you think you responded in this way?
- "They knew the story was about them." Do you think they knew it at the beginning, in the middle, near the end, or somewhere else? Why do you think that?
- If you were the owner of the vineyard, would you come and "clean house"?
- Although justice is eventually served in this story, don't miss the mercy: "He sent another. . . . And on and on, many others." Is that what you would have done if you were the owner of the vineyard? What does this say about God's mercy?

READ

From *Wild at Heart*, by John Eldredge[1]

This is the world he has made. This is the world that is still going on. And he doesn't walk away from the mess we've made of it. Now he lives, almost cheerfully, certainly heroically, in a dynamic relationship with us and with our world. "Then the Lord intervened" is perhaps the single most common phrase about him in Scripture, in one form or another. Look at the stories he writes. There's the one where the children of Israel are pinned against the Red Sea, no way out, with Pharaoh and his army barreling down on them in murderous fury. Then God shows up. There's Shadrach, Meshach, and Abednego, who get rescued only *after* they're thrown into the fiery furnace. Then God shows up. He lets the mob kill Jesus, bury him . . . then he shows up. Do you know why God loves writing such incredible stories? Because *he loves to come through.* He loves to show us he has what it takes.

It's not the nature of God to limit his risks and cover his bases. Far from it. Most of the time, he actually lets the odds stack up against him. Against Goliath, a seasoned soldier and a trained killer, he sends . . . a freckle-faced little shepherd kid with a slingshot. Most commanders going into battle want as many infantry as they can get. God cuts Gideon's army from thirty-two thousand to three hundred. Then he equips the ragtag little band that's left with torches and watering pots. It's not just a battle or two that God takes his chances with, either. Have you thought about his handling of the gospel? God needs to get a message out to the human race, without which they will perish . . . forever. What's the plan? First, he starts with the most unlikely group ever: a couple of prostitutes, a few fishermen with no better than a second-grade education, a tax collector. Then, he passes the ball to us. Unbelievable.

God's relationship with us and with our world is just that: a *relationship.* As with every relationship, there's a certain amount of unpredictability, and the ever-present likelihood that you'll get hurt.

THINK

"What do you think the owner of the vineyard will do?"

- What is your response to Eldredge's words?
- Do you believe God really "loves to come through"? Why or why not?
- Think about a time when God clearly came through for you—but came through *later* than your preferred timing. Describe it in detail.
- How did that experience leave you feeling about God?

READ

From *Bold Love*, by Dr. Dan B. Allender and Dr. Tremper Longman III[2]

In her book *Pilgrim at Tinker Creek*, Annie Dillard paints a frightening, and yet thoroughly comforting, picture of God's otherness:

> There is not a guarantee in the world. Oh your needs are guaranteed, your needs are absolutely guaranteed by the most stringent of warranties, in the plainest, truest words: knock, seek, ask. But you must read the fine print. "Not as the world giveth, give I unto you." That's the catch. If you can catch it it will catch you up, aloft, up to any gap at all, and you'll come back, for you will come back, transformed in a way you may not have bargained for—dribbling and crazed. The waters of separation, however lightly sprinkled, leave indelible stains. Did you think, before you were caught, that you needed, say, life? Do you think you will keep your life, or anything else you love? But no. Your needs are all met. But not as the world giveth. You see the needs of your own spirit met whenever you have asked, and you have learned that the outrageous guarantee holds. You see the creatures die, and you know you will die. And one day it occurs to you that you must not need life. Obviously. And then you're gone. You have finally understood that you're dealing with a maniac.[3]

Many Christians will undoubtedly be put off, if not offended, by the use of the term *maniac* to describe God. But honesty requires us to admit that that's how He seems. Talk to Job. His God struck a bargain with Satan to see how faithful Job would be. Job is found to be without sin in the normal sense of the word, but out of an imperfect heart he develops a malignant, slow-growing, self-justified rage at God. God, then, intervenes in a violent storm and exposes Job by His pointed, probing, sarcastic power. Then Job repents. Why? Because he sees God, after having spit in His face.

Silence, in its life-changing power, comes to those who see the darkness of their own heart in light of the holy standards of God. Even more, they see the reflection of their hatred in the still tender eyes of God. The miracle of grace—really, the wonder of God's character—produces the miracle of our change. A sight of God's holiness without a hint of His mercy will lead to either hopeless despair or to something even more awful, a pharisaical presumption of ability to "do His will." On the other hand, a mouthful of mercy without a somber taste of holiness seems to move us to a brazen familiarity with deity that twists Him into everyone's favorite uncle. Such intimacy is sloppy and undignified, and it eventually leads us to paint God with colors of our own making. The Bible portrays God in ways that ought to stun us.

THINK   "What do you think the owner of the vineyard will do?"

- Go back and underline words or phrases in this passage that spoke to you.
- Why did these certain words or phrases catch your attention? Do you agree with them? Do they bother you?
- Have you ever considered God a maniac? Don't worry, there is no electric-shock button hooked up to this question. Just think about it in light of the ways God has worked in your life.
- What is your response to these words: "A sight of God's holiness without a hint of His mercy will lead to either hopeless despair or to something even more awful, a pharisaical presumption of ability to 'do His will.' On the other hand, a mouthful of mercy without a somber taste of holiness seems to move us to a brazen familiarity with deity that twists Him into everyone's favorite uncle"?
- Where would you place yourself in relation to God? Hopeless despair? Pharisaical presumption? Brazen familiarity?

THINK (continued)

READ

Job 3:1-10,20-26

Then Job broke the silence. He spoke up and cursed his fate:

"Obliterate the day I was born.
    Blank out the night I was conceived!
Let it be a black hole in space.
    May God above forget it ever happened.
    Erase it from the books!
May the day of my birth be buried in deep darkness,
    shrouded by the fog,
    swallowed by the night.
And the night of my conception—the devil take it!
    Rip the date off the calendar,
    delete it from the almanac.
Oh, turn that night into pure nothingness—
    no sounds of pleasure from that night, ever!
May those who are good at cursing curse that day.
    Unleash the sea beast, Leviathan, on it.
May its morning stars turn to black cinders,
    waiting for a daylight that never comes,
    never once seeing the first light of dawn.
And why? Because it released me from my mother's womb
    into a life with so much trouble. . . .

"Why does God bother giving light to the miserable,
    why bother keeping bitter people alive,
Those who want in the worst way to die, and can't,
    who can't imagine anything better than death,
Who count the day of their death and burial
    the happiest day of their life?
What's the point of life when it doesn't make sense,
    when God blocks all the roads to meaning?

"Instead of bread I get groans for my supper,
then leave the table and vomit my anguish.
The worst of my fears has come true,
what I've dreaded most has happened.
My repose is shattered, my peace destroyed.
No rest for me, ever—death has invaded life."

THINK   "What do you think the owner of the vineyard will do?"

- Have you or others you've known ever been at this Job-point?
- Were you or they thinking that the owner of the vineyard should or could have done something to help? Did he?
- Have you ever had thoughts like these from Job 29:1-6?

Oh, how I long for the good old days,
when God took such very good care of me.
He always held a lamp before me
and I walked through the dark by its light.
Oh, how I miss those golden years
when God's friendship graced my home,
When the Mighty One was still by my side
and my children were all around me,
When everything was going my way,
and nothing seemed too difficult.

- What prompted those thoughts? How did you deal with them?

READ

From *Pilgrim at Tinker Creek*, by Annie Dillard[4]

Thomas Merton wrote, "There is always a temptation to diddle around in the contemplative life, making itsy-bitsy statues." There is always an enormous temptation in all of life to diddle around making itsy-bitsy friends and meals and journeys for itsy-bitsy years on end. It is so self-conscious, so apparently moral, simply to step aside from the gaps where the creeks and winds pour down, saying, I never merited this grace, quite rightly, and then to sulk along the rest of your days on the edge of rage. I won't have it. The world is wilder than that in all directions, more dangerous and bitter, more extravagant and bright. We are making hay when we should be making whoopee; we are raising tomatoes when we should be raising Cain, or Lazarus.

Ezekiel excoriates false prophets as those who have "not gone up into the gaps." The gaps are the thing. The gaps are the spirit's one home, the altitudes and latitudes so dazzlingly spare and clean that the spirit can discover itself for the first time like a once-blind man unbound. The gaps are the clifts in the rock where you cower to see the back parts of God; they are the fissures between mountains and cells the wind lances through, the icy narrowing fiords splitting the cliffs of mystery. Go up into the gaps. If you can find them; they shift and vanish too. Stalk the gaps. Squeak into a gap in the soil, turn, and unlock—more than a maple—a universe. This is how you spend this afternoon, and tomorrow morning, and tomorrow afternoon. *Spend* the afternoon. You can't take it with you.

THINK   "What do you think the owner of the vineyard will do?"

- Do you know anyone (maybe even you) who is sulking along the rest of his or her days "on the edge of rage"? What prompts that sulking?

- When the owner of the vineyard doesn't do what we expect, it leaves a gap. But according to Dillard, "The gaps are the thing. The gaps are the spirit's one home, the altitudes and latitudes so dazzlingly spare and clean that the spirit can discover itself for the first time like a once-blind man unbound." What would it look like for you to "go up into the gaps"?
- Are you in any way afraid of what you might find? Why?

PRAY

Look back at the "Think" sections. Ruminate on your responses. Let them distill into a prayer, and then write that prayer below.

Dangerous Lover . . .

The issue of prayer is not prayer; the issue of prayer is God.

ABRAHAM HESCHEL

LIVE   "What do you think the owner of the vineyard will do?"

The challenge now is to take this question further along—to live out this question. Think of one thing, *just one*, that you can personally do to wrestle with the question, inhabit the character of it, and live it in everyday life. In the following space, jot down your thoughts on this "one thing." Read the Scripture and quotes that follow for additional inspiration. During the coming week, pray about this "one thing," talk with a close friend about it, and learn to live the question.

One thing . . .

I admit I once lived by rumors of you;
   now I have it all firsthand—from my own eyes and ears!
I'm sorry—forgive me. I'll never do that again, I promise!
   I'll never again live on crusts of hearsay, crumbs of rumor.
                                                    Job 42:5-6

Whatever your end may be, accept my amazement.
May I stand until death forever at attention
for any your least instruction or enlightenment.
I even feel sure you will assist me again, Master of insight & beauty.

                                                    John Berryman

Live the questions now. Perhaps you will then gradually, without noticing it, live along some distant day into the answer.
RAINER MARIA RILKE, *LETTERS TO A YOUNG POET*

"Don't you ever read the Bible?" (Mark 12:26)

Before You Begin

Take some time to reflect and prepare your heart and mind
for this study. Read the following Scripture passage. Soak
up God's Word. There's no hurry. Then, when you're ready,
turn the page and begin.

Psalm 119:97-104

Oh, how I love all you've revealed;
  I reverently ponder it all the day long.
Your commands give me an edge on my enemies;
  they never become obsolete.
I've even become smarter than my teachers
  since I've pondered and absorbed your counsel.
I've become wiser than the wise old sages
  simply by doing what you tell me.
I watch my step, avoiding the ditches and ruts of evil
  so I can spend all my time keeping your Word.
I never make detours from the route you laid out;
  you gave me such good directions.
Your words are so choice, so tasty;
  I prefer them to the best home cooking.
With your instruction, I understand life;
  that's why I hate false propaganda.

READ

Mark 12:18-27

Some Sadducees, the party that denies any possibility of resurrection, came up and asked, "Teacher, Moses wrote that if a man dies and leaves a wife but no child, his brother is obligated to marry the widow and have children. Well, there once were seven brothers. The first took a wife. He died childless. The second married her. He died, and still no child. The same with the third. All seven took their turn, but no child. Finally the wife died. When they are raised at the resurrection, whose wife is she? All seven were her husband."

Jesus said, "You're way off base, and here's why: One, you don't know your Bibles; two, you don't know how God works. After the dead are raised up, we're past the marriage business. As it is with angels now, all our ecstasies and intimacies then will be with God. And regarding the dead, whether or not they are raised, **don't you ever read the Bible**? How God at the bush said to Moses, 'I am—not *was*—the God of Abraham, the God of Isaac, and the God of Jacob'? The living God is God of the *living*, not the dead. You're way, way off base."

THINK   "Don't you ever read the Bible?"

- What is your immediate response to this question?
- Why do you think you responded in this way?
- Put the sincerity or insincerity of the Sadducees aside for a moment. Have you ever wondered about the question they posed to Jesus?
- "After the dead are raised up, we're past the marriage business. As it is with angels now, all our ecstasies and intimacies then will be with God." What is your reaction to these words of Jesus? How do they make you feel?

- Put yourself in the Sadducees' sandals for a moment. You asked a question and Jesus replied, "You don't know your Bibles." Do you think you would have heard anything else he said after that statement?
- Do you believe in the Resurrection?

READ

From *A Prayer for Owen Meany*, by John Irving[1]

Toronto: April 12, 1987—a rainy Palm Sunday. It is not a warm spring rain—not a "seasonal" rain, as my grandmother liked to say. It is a raw cold rain, a suitable day for the Passion of Our Lord Jesus Christ. At Grace Church on-the-Hill, the children and the acolytes stood huddled in the narthex; holding their palm fronds, they resembled tourists who'd landed in the tropics on an unseasonably cold day. The organist chose Brahms for the processional—"*O Welt ich muss dich lassen*"; "O world I must leave you."

Owen hated Palm Sunday: the treachery of Judas, the cowardice of Peter, the weakness of Pilate.

"IT'S BAD ENOUGH THAT THEY CRUCIFIED HIM," Owen said, "BUT THEY MADE FUN OF HIM, TOO!"

Canon Mackie read heavily from Matthew: how they mocked Jesus, how they spit on him, how he cried, "My God, my God, why hast thou forsaken me?"

I find that Holy Week is draining; no matter how many times I have lived through his crucifixion, my anxiety about his resurrection is undiminished—I am terrified that, this year, it won't happen; that, that year, it didn't. Anyone can be sentimental about the Nativity; any fool can feel like a Christian at Christmas. But Easter is the main event; if you don't believe in the resurrection, you're not a believer.

"IF YOU DON'T BELIEVE IN EASTER," Owen Meany said, "DON'T KID YOURSELF—DON'T CALL YOURSELF A CHRISTIAN."

Toronto: April 19, 1987—a humid, summery Easter Sunday. It does not matter what prelude begins the service; I will always hear Handel's *Messiah*—and my mother's not-quite-trained soprano singing, "I know that my Redeemer liveth."

This morning, in Grace Church on-the-Hill, I sat very still, waiting for that passage in John; I knew what was coming. In the old King James version, it was called a "sepulchre"; in the Revised Standard version, it is just a "tomb." Either way, I know the story by heart.

"Now on the first day of the week Mary Magdalene came to the tomb early, while it was still dark, and saw that the stone had been taken away from the tomb. So she ran, and went to Simon Peter and the other disciple, the one whom Jesus loved, and said to them, 'They have taken the Lord out of the tomb, and we do not know where they have laid him.'"

I remember what Owen used to say about that passage; every Easter, he would lean against me in the pew and whisper into my ear. "THIS IS THE PART THAT ALWAYS GIVES ME THE SHIVERS."

THINK   "Don't you ever read the Bible?"

- What is your response to this excerpt (particularly Owen's response to the Bible passage)?
- Owen Meany was a strong believer in the Resurrection. But he still got the shivers. Are there parts of the Resurrection story that give you the shivers? If so, describe them.
- What kind of belief or lack of belief in the Resurrection were you given as a child? Who or where did it come from?

READ

1 Corinthians 15:12-34

Now, let me ask you something profound yet troubling. If you became believers because you trusted the proclamation that Christ is alive, risen from the dead, how can you let people say that there is no such thing as a resurrection? If there's no resurrection, there's no living Christ. And face it—if there's no resurrection for Christ, everything we've told you is smoke and mirrors, and everything you've staked your life on is smoke and mirrors. Not only that, but we would be guilty of telling a string of barefaced lies about God, all these affidavits we passed on to you verifying that God raised up Christ—sheer fabrications, if there's no resurrection.

If corpses can't be raised, then Christ wasn't, because he was indeed dead. And if Christ weren't raised, then all you're doing is wandering about in the dark, as lost as ever. It's even worse for those who died hoping in Christ and resurrection, because they're already in their graves. If all we get out of Christ is a little inspiration for a few short years, we're a pretty sorry lot. But the truth is that Christ *has* been raised up, the first in a long legacy of those who are going to leave the cemeteries.

There is a nice symmetry in this: Death initially came by a man, and resurrection from death came by a man. Everybody dies in Adam; everybody comes alive in Christ. But we have to wait our turn: Christ is first, then those with him at his Coming, the grand consummation when, after crushing the opposition, he hands over his kingdom to God the Father. He won't let up until the last enemy is down—and the very last enemy is death! As the psalmist said, "He laid them low, one and all; he walked all over them." When Scripture says that "he walked all over them," it's obvious that he couldn't at the same time be walked on. When everything and everyone is finally under God's rule, the Son will step down, taking his place with everyone else, showing that God's rule is absolutely comprehensive—a perfect ending!

Why do you think people offer themselves to be baptized for those already in the grave? If there's no chance of resurrection for a corpse, if God's power stops at the cemetery gates, why do we keep doing things that suggest he's going to clean the place out someday, pulling everyone up on their feet alive?

And why do you think I keep risking my neck in this dangerous work? I look death in the face practically every day I live. Do you think I'd do this if I wasn't convinced of your resurrection and mine as guaranteed by the resurrected Messiah Jesus? Do you think I was just trying to act heroic when I fought the wild beasts at Ephesus, hoping it wouldn't be the end of me? Not on your life! It's resurrection, resurrection, always resurrection, that undergirds what I do and say, the way I live. If there's no resurrection, "We eat, we drink, the next day we die," and that's all there is to it. But don't fool yourselves. Don't let yourselves be poisoned by this anti-resurrection loose talk. "Bad company ruins good manners."

Think straight. Awaken to the holiness of life. No more playing fast and loose with resurrection facts. Ignorance of God is a luxury you can't afford in times like these.

THINK   "Don't you ever read the Bible?"

- Jesus said the Sadducees didn't know their Bibles or how God worked. Think again about Paul's words in this passage: "It's resurrection, resurrection, always resurrection, that undergirds what I do and say, the way I live." God works by resurrection. And for Paul, this wasn't merely an intellectual theorem. It penetrated how he lived. Does that truth undergird what you do and say, the way you live? If so, give at least one example of this.
- Think about this: Paul used two words to describe his resurrection-based living: *risky* and *dangerous*. If a friend or coworker were to describe you, would either of these words surface in the description? Explain.

THINK (continued)

READ

From *The Divine Conspiracy*, by Dallas Willard[2]

Discussing his own upcoming death with his friends, he says to them, "If you loved me, you would be happy because I go to the Father, where I am better off than here" (John 14:28). In different wording, "I go to the Father, and my Father is greater than I." Nothing for *him* to grieve about in that! Of course it left his friends with much sorrow *for themselves*, which is understandable and appropriate. But they should also rejoice for him at the same time.

And of course this all accords perfectly with his response to the faith of the thief dying with him: "Today you and I will be together in a wonderful place, Paradise" (Luke 23:43). This statement could only be a falsehood if it meant anything less than that the thief would be very much himself, in fine shape, in a wonderful situation with Jesus and, no doubt, with others as well.

Such is the understanding of the New Testament as a whole. Those who live in reliance upon the word and person of Jesus, and know by experience the reality of his kingdom, are always better off "dead," from the personal point of view. Paul's language is, "to die is gain" (Phil. 1:21). And again: "To depart and be with Christ is very much better" than to remain here (v. 23). We remain willing, of course, to stay at our position here to serve others at God's appointment. But we live in the knowledge that, as Paul elsewhere says, "Jesus the Anointed has abolished death and has, through the gospel, made life and immortality obvious" (2 Timothy 1:10).

THINK   *"Don't you ever read the Bible?"*

- Think about this: The Sadducees didn't have "the New Testament as a whole" to understand. But they did have the "word and person of Jesus," the fulfillment of all the Scriptures, right in front of them. Why do you think they missed him?

- "'To depart and be with Christ is very much better' than to remain here." What is your response to these words? Do you agree or disagree?
- Can you think of some ways other than his death in which Jesus has "made life and immortality obvious"?

READ

From *Lament for a Son*, by Nicholas Wolterstorff[3]

"Blessed are those who mourn." What can it mean? One can understand why Jesus hails those who hunger and thirst for righteousness, why he hails the merciful, why he hails the pure in heart, why he hails the peacemakers, why he hails those who endure under persecution. These are qualities of character which belong to the life of the kingdom. But why does he hail the mourners of the world? Why cheer tears? It must be that mourning is also a quality of character that belongs to the life of his realm.

Who then are the mourners? The mourners are those who have caught a glimpse of God's new day, who ache with all their being for that day's coming, and who break out into tears when confronted with its absence. They are the ones who realize that in God's realm of peace there is no one blind and who ache whenever they see someone unseeing. They are the ones who realize that in God's realm there is no one hungry and who ache whenever they see someone starving. They are the ones who realize that in God's realm there is no one falsely accused and who ache whenever they see someone imprisoned unjustly. They are the ones who realize that in God's realm there is no one who fails to see God and who ache whenever they see someone unbelieving. They are the ones who realize that in God's realm there is no one who suffers oppression and who ache whenever they see someone beat down. They are the ones who realize that in God's realm there is no one without dignity and who ache whenever they see someone treated with indignity. They are the ones who realize that in God's realm of peace there is neither death nor tears and who ache whenever they see someone crying tears over death. The mourners are aching visionaries.

Such people Jesus blesses; he hails them, he praises them, he salutes them. And he gives them the promise that the new day for whose absence they ache will come. They will be comforted.

The Stoics of antiquity said: Be calm. Disengage yourself. Neither laugh nor weep. Jesus says: Be open to the wounds of the world. Mourn humanity's mourning, weep over humanity's weeping, be wounded by humanity's wounds, be in agony over humanity's agony. But do so in the good cheer that a day of peace is coming.

THINK   "Don't you ever read the Bible?"

- Re-read Wolterstorff's words. They alone are worth whatever you paid for this book.
- Have you ever considered the idea that mourning complements a belief in the Resurrection? Why or why not?
- Recall the last time you ached when you saw someone in a negative situation. Describe it in detail.
- Think about this: Christians are sometimes accused of being "so heavenly minded that they're no earthly good." Being an "aching visionary"—understanding that God works in resurrection and at the same time being open to the wounds of the world—is a remedy to that.

PRAY

Look back at the "Think" sections. Ruminate on your responses.
Let them distill into a prayer, and then write that prayer below.

Alpha and Omega . . .

The issue of prayer is not prayer; the issue of prayer is God.

ABRAHAM HESCHEL

LIVE

"Don't you ever read the Bible?"

The challenge now is to take this question further along—to live out this question. Think of one thing, *just one*, that you can personally do to wrestle with the question, inhabit the character of it, and live it in everyday life. In the following space, jot down your thoughts on this "one thing." Read the Scripture and quotes that follow for additional inspiration. During the coming week, pray about this "one thing," talk with a close friend about it, and learn to live the question.

One thing...

Our old age is the scorching of the bush
By life's indwelling, incorruptible blaze.
O life, burn at this feeble shell of me,
Till I the sore singed garment off shall push,
Flap out my Psyche wings, and to thee rush.

George MacDonald

"Look! I'm making everything new. Write it all down—each word dependable and accurate."
    Then he said, "It's happened. I'm A to Z. I'm the Beginning, I'm the Conclusion."

Revelation 21:5-6

Live the questions now. Perhaps you will then gradually, without noticing it, live along some distant day into the answer.
RAINER MARIA RILKE, *LETTERS TO A YOUNG POET*

NOTES

LESSON 1

1. Tilden Edwards, *Spiritual Friend: Reclaiming the Gift of Spiritual Direction* (Ramsey, NJ: Paulist, 1980), 74.
2. Karen Mains, *Making Sunday Special* (Carmel, NY: Guideposts, 1987), 22–23.
3. Jean Vanier, *Community and Growth* (Mahwah, NJ: Paulist, 1989), 177.
4. Marva Dawn, *Keeping the Sabbath Wholly: Ceasing, Resting, Embracing, Feasting* (Grand Rapids, MI: Eerdmans, 1989), 119, 122.

LESSON 2

1. Frederick Buechner, *The Clown in the Belfry: Writings on Faith and Fiction* (New York: HarperCollins, 1992), 130–131.
2. Walter Wangerin Jr., *Ragman and Other Cries of Faith* (New York: HarperCollins, 1984), 73–74.
3. John Eldredge, *Waking the Dead: The Glory of a Heart Fully Alive* (Nashville: Nelson, 2003), 23–25.
4. Ken Gire, *Reflections on the Movies: Hearing God in the Unlikeliest of Places* (Colorado Springs, CO: Chariot/Victor, 2000), 70–71.

LESSON 3

1. Helmut Thielicke, *Life Can Begin Again: Sermons on the Sermon on the Mount* (Philadelphia: Fortress, 1963), 140–143.
2. John Eldredge, *The Journey of Desire: Searching for the Life We've Only Dreamed Of* (Nashville: Nelson, 2000), 199–200.

LESSON 4

1. Rainer Maria Rilke, *Letters to a Young Poet* (New York: Norton, 1954), 19–20.
2. Jean Vanier, *Community and Growth* (Mahwah, NJ: Paulist, 1989), 194.
3. David Whyte, *Crossing the Unknown Sea: Work As a Pilgrimage of Identity* (New York: Riverhead Books, 2001), 185–186.
4. "Loaves and Fishes" from *The House of Belonging* by David Whyte. Copyright © 1997 by David Whyte. Used by permission of the author and Many Rivers Press.

LESSON 5

1. Thomas Merton, *New Seeds of Contemplation* (New York: New Directions Publishing, 1972), 22–24.
2. Dave Tomlinson, *The Post-Evangelical* (London: Society for Promoting Christian Knowledge, 1995), 43–44.
3. Walter Wangerin Jr., *Little Lamb, Who Made Thee? A Book About Children and Parents* (Grand Rapids, MI: Zondervan, 1993), 179–183.

LESSON 6

1. Walter Wangerin Jr., *The Orphean Passages: The Drama of Faith* (Grand Rapids, MI: Zondervan, 1996), 9, 12–13.
2. Annie Dillard, *Teaching a Stone to Talk: Expeditions and Encounters* (New York: Harper & Row, 1982), 95.
3. Philip Yancey, *The Jesus I Never Knew* (Grand Rapids, MI: Zondervan, 1995), 177–178.

LESSON 7

1. N. T. Wright, *The Challenge of Jesus: Rediscovering Who Jesus Was and Is* (Downers Grove, IL: InterVarsity, 1999), 14–15.
2. C. S. Lewis, *God in the Dock: Essays on Theology and Ethics* (Grand Rapids, MI: Eerdmans, 1970), 156.
3. Lewis, 158.
4. G. K. Chesterton, *Orthodoxy: The Romance of Faith* (New York: Bantam Doubleday Dell, 1990), 146–147.

LESSON 8

1. Norman Maclean, *A River Runs Through It and Other Stories* (Chicago: University of Chicago Press, 1976), 7–9.
2. Mitch Albom, *Tuesdays with Morrie: An Old Man, a Young Man, and Life's Greatest Lesson* (New York: Bantam Doubleday Dell, 1997), 159.
3. Eugene H. Peterson, *Where Your Treasure Is: Psalms That Summon You from Self to Community* (Grand Rapids, MI: Eerdmans, 1993), 94–95.

LESSON 9

1. John Eldredge, *Wild at Heart: Discovering the Passionate Soul of a Man* (Nashville: Nelson, 2001), 31–32.
2. Dr. Dan B. Allender and Dr. Tremper Longman III, *Bold Love* (Colorado Springs, CO: NavPress, 1992), 73–74.
3. Annie Dillard, *Pilgrim at Tinker Creek* (New York: Harper & Row, 1974), 269–270.
4. Dillard, 268–269.

LESSON 10

1. John Irving, *A Prayer for Owen Meany* (New York: Morrow, 1989), 281–282.
2. Dallas Willard, *The Divine Conspiracy: Rediscovering Our Hidden Life in God* (New York: HarperCollins, 1998), 394.
3. Nicholas Wolterstorff, *Lament for a Son* (Grand Rapids, MI: Eerdmans, 1987), 84–86.

GROW STRONGER IN YOUR FAITH BY WRESTLING WITH LIFE'S BIGGEST QUESTIONS.

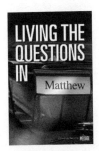

Living the Questions in Matthew
1-57683-833-1

Living the Questions in Luke
1-57683-861-7

Living the Questions in John
1-57683-834-X

Jesus asked more questions than he ever answered outright. Now readers and study groups can wrestle with some of these issues with these intriguing new studies of the Gospels based on *The Message*—the eye-opening translation by Eugene Peterson. Through these compelling studies, readers can embrace life's questions and build a stronger faith.

Visit your local Christian bookstore,
call NavPress at 1-800-366-7788, or log on to www.navpress.com
to purchase.

To locate a Christian bookstore near you, call 1-800-991-7747.

NAVPRESS
BRINGING TRUTH TO LIFE
www.navpress.com